Back to the Zone

Back
to the
Zone

Sport and Inner Experiences

Damien Lafont, PhD

BREAKAWAY BOOKS
HALCOTTSVILLE, NEW YORK
2012

ISBN: 978-1-891369-99-7
Library of Congress Control Number: 2012948804

Published by Breakaway Books
P.O. Box 24
Halcottsville, NY 12438
www.breakawaybooks.com

10 9 8 7 6 5 4 3 2 1

to Judith

Contents

Acknowledgments

My deepest appreciation to the following people who contributed, directly or indirectly, to this book: Michael Murphy, Gilles Goetgebuhr, Jean Brechbuhl, Terry Orlick, Tim Gallwey, Michael Lardon, Fiona Taylor, Roy Palmer, Jacob Liberman, Phil Jackson, Ronan Lafaix, John Douillard, Peter Spang, Jim Taylor, Jerry Lynch, Fran Pirozzolo, Hélène Grimaud, George Leonard, Jean-Philippe Vaillant, Christy Frikken, Scott Ford, Costas Karageorghis, Virginie Van Wassenhove, Geoff Mangum, Joe Parent, Julie Bouteraon, Andy Clark, Thomas Sorensen, Charlie Jones, and Natalie Atkinson. Thank you to all the inspiring athletes who are quoted in this book, for sharing intimate details of their journeys: Fiona Taylor, Drew Ginn, Pete Sampras, Roger Federer, Mark Allen, Chris Evert, Billie Jean King, Arthur Ashe. Thanks also to the body–mind masters, past and present, who lighted the way: Lao-tzu, Daisetz Suzuki, Kazumi Tabata, Bruce Lee. A very big thank-you to my great teachers Dan Millman and James

Redfield for the ways in which you have inspired me and enriched my perspective, my life, and the thoughts shared in *Back to the Zone*! I would also like to thank my past coaches, Jean Pierre Ricard, Guylain Condroyer, and Thierry Celier-Barette. A big thank-you to family members Claude Lafont, Xavier Lafont, Zachary Taylor, and Xander Taylor for their love and support. Finally, I would like to extend my heartfelt thanks to my wife, Judith, for the wonderful gift of love and support she gives me. Judith, thank you for making my dreams come true.

Part One

In the Zone

We now hope that someone working with people who are actively engaged in sport will gather first-hand examples of metanormal experiences to create a larger and more comprehensive collection.

—Michael Murphy and Rhea White, *In the Zone,* 1995

Welcome to the Zone

You unlock this door with the key of imagination. Beyond is another dimension. A dimension of sound. A dimension of sight. A dimension of mind. You're moving into a land of both shadow and substance, of things and ideas. You just crossed over into the Twilight Zone.

—Rod Serling, *The Twilight Zone*

Men and women have reported similar experiences in many very different sports: sensations of speed and power; out-of-the-ordinary moments of deep well-being, wonder, ecstasy, control, peace, tranquility; instinctive action; feelings of unity, detachment, floating, lightness, and freedom; even a sense of immortality!

"The Zone is the essence of the athletic experience, and those moments of going beyond yourself are the underlying allure of sport," says Dave Meggyesy, former pro football player. Athletes tell us that in the Zone, you do not fight against yourself, you're not afraid, and you live in the moment, in a special place and time.

The Zone—better known in the United States than in Europe, where its study is new—is a universal experience lived by athletes in all disciplines. Some speak of flow, peak experience, being on autopilot, white moments, or being in a bubble. Throughout this book I will use the term *Zone*,[1] because, as we shall see, this term with its rich ambiguity and its many meanings is more than a reference to an unknown place!

Some attribute the term *Zone* to tennis champion Arthur Ashe, who once stated he was "playing in the Zone." However nobody really knows who first used the expression. What *is* certain is that this is a relatively new term in the lexicon of sports culture.

Throughout this book, our pursuit of the Zone will take us on a world tour to meet some characters who have dedicated their lives to this extraordinary human experience. We'll see the Zone not only through the eyes of psychologists but also through those of the athletes and coaches who experience it directly.

I remember:
my best experiences;
my best performances;
my best feelings.

White moments

Sport is really a matter of chills.

—Jean Dion

All great athletes know "that" feeling. Almost all of them, in their own way, are seeking it. They are masters in their field, they know their bodies perfectly, and yet they find the Zone difficult to describe.

Our understanding of the Zone comes through carefully observing and listening to these great champions. Their experiences of this hidden world can often be captured during interviews. It's true! Athlete interviews are both insightful and instructive, and champions can teach us a lot if we take the time to listen.

If the term is recent, however, the experience is definitely not. Still, athletes rarely spoke about it until recently, perhaps feeling a little strange and finding the subject too personal. The topic was somewhat taboo, and athletes weren't ready to break the unwritten rule of silence.

Several years ago Scott Ostler, a sports reporter at the *San Francisco Chronicle,* attempted to explore the topic with athletes. He often faced cold silences. His strange questions regarding the inner experience of sports was what author Andrew Cooper referred to in *Playing in the Zone* as a hidden dimension or "secret life."[2] Over the last ten years the situation has evolved, but even today *the Zone* is a cliché for many athletes and sports journalists, and its true meaning remains elusive. We often hear about people who report having been in the Zone, but we still do not know what that *really* means.[3]

Tennis champion Billie Jean King describes it as "a perfect combination of violent action taking place in an atmosphere of total tranquility. When it happens I want to stop the match and grab the microphone and shout, 'That's what it's all about.' It's not the big prize I'm going to win at the end of the match, or anything else. It's just having done something that's totally pure and having experienced the perfect emotion, and I'm always sad that I can't communicate that feeling right at the moment it's happening. I can only hope people realize what's going on."

Most of those who have touched it at least once say, "This is what's all about." But what is it about? Surely not just sport!

Sportscaster Charlie Jones, in his book *What Makes Winners Win,* paints a beautiful picture: "The Zone is the perfect day. The smiles are larger, the heart is fuller, and the sunset is more beautiful. Unfortunately, we're not allowed to visit the Zone every day."[4]

Think of your past:
Have you had extraordinary experiences?
What did you feel? What did you think?
Have you tried to live these moments again?

Take the time to read *In the Zone* by Michael Murphy and Rhea White.

I open my mind to all possibilities.

Optimal Zone

If professional athletes seem reluctant to tell us more, many of those who gravitate to sports—including writers, researchers, psychologists, and amateur athletes—are much less so! In 1989, an article in *The New York Times Magazine*[5] reported that the Zone has been studied by psychologists, neuroscientists, and anthropologists, among others. It was explained through the lens of various disciplines, from genetics to environment, motivation, hypnosis, and even parapsychology. Today sports psychologists utilize methods such as visualization, motivation, and psychotherapy to help their clients achieve the Zone more easily.

Let's review the two main theories describing the optimal psychological state known as the Zone. Two pioneers in sports psychology have dedicated their lives to studying this state. Hungarian professor Mihaly Czikszentmihalyi first introduced the concept of flow in 1975, and Yuri Hanin Russian professor—proposed the 1980 theory of the Individual Zone of Optimal Functioning (IZOF). *Flow* is best defined as a perfect correspondence between the demands of the activity and the capacity of the athlete. During flow, the athlete loses all sense of conscious self-awareness and become completely absorbed in the task at hand. This creates a condition in which the performance is fully enjoyable and rewarding by itself. Czikszentmihalyi refers to flow as an *autotelic* experience, from the Greek words *auto,* meaning "self," and *telos,* which means "goal" or "end." Thus, an autotelic experiment is an end in itself or intrinsically rewarding. This concept highlights the pleasure that comes from participation rather than extrinsic feedback, such as medals, trophies, or public recognition.

The theory of Yuri Hanin, who led Finland's Research Institute for Olympic Sports, is a little different: He assumes that each athlete has an optimal zone of arousal or "competitive anxiety" from which he performs at his peak. If the anxiety of the athlete leaves the Zone, the level of performance decreases.

If these theories do not provide the keys to enter the Zone, they are nonetheless useful in helping us to adjust our level of anxiety (mental and physical) and identify key psychological components of the flow we seek to develop.

Be aware.

Develop awareness of your levels
of stress and anxiety.

*Nothing external has any power over me.
I feel my inner strength.*

The features

Mind is the key. But where is the key to the mind?
—Sir John Whitmore

There are many examples of the Zone, but it still seems difficult to articulate what it is. The athletes willing to testify are rather evasive, and the concepts and theories explaining these out-of-the-norm experiences have yet to be fully explored. Sports psychologists are still trying to define and describe the features that epitomize the Zone.

Numerous studies have been conducted in our efforts to better understand these experiences. Some researchers have simply interviewed athletes, asking them to recall the feelings and sensations they experienced during great moments of competition. Others compare the psychological characteristics of winning athletes with those of athletes who fail. Our understanding also involves the testimonials of coaches who observe these experiments.

Dr. Sarah McIntyre, a sports psychologist with the University of Sydney, says that before seeking to enter the Zone we must have a clear idea of what this state really is. What are the physical, cognitive, and perceptual states related to this Zone? Does being in the Zone confer any benefits, and can other factors bring these same benefits? Alternatively, do these factors always lead us into the Zone? These are some of the questions researcher Susan Jackson focused on when she sought to identify the conditions that may allow us to reach the Zone by controlling the mind. For her, although the contexts may differ greatly, athletes' experiences of total absorption share some common characteristics.

Common Characteristics of the Zone Experience

BALANCE

Reaching the Zone requires finding the right balance between the challenge and our skills. This is less a matter of our talent, and more a matter of our *perception* of it.

PERCEPTION

What we think we can achieve will determine our experience more than our actual abilities will. To change our perception of any given situation requires self-confidence and can be further developed by thinking about past successes rather than failures.

However, as noted by Bill Walton—a former Boston Celtics player—the challenge of an opponent can also ignite heightened mental states. "What you do is try to re-create the same situation every time in the game through a routine, the timing of your lunch before the match, getting dressed, your thoughts, your nap, your whole day. But what really brings it is the intensity of your game and also to know that the opponent can beat you." For some, reaching the Zone seems to be easier when a task is more demanding than usual and they are required to give more of themselves. If it's too easy they get bored; if it's too difficult, they become anxious. The Zone is thus blocked by boredom and anxiety.

TOTAL ABSORPTION

Taking the external elements as they are means we can focus on the process and enter into total absorption. This state is a cohesive and balanced fusion between action and consciousness. Such a union between mental and physical processes creates an acute sense of movement, resulting in perfect timing. In the Zone, movement requires little effort.

CLARITY

A simple but imperative aspect of any high-performance state is clarity. It is important to have clear goals. You can link these goals with words, feelings, or pictures of success. In the short term, goals are useful to maintain focus on the action, not on results. They also help provide a positive direction for attention.

FEEDBACK

Feedback is essential for a successful performance. The feedback that athletes can plug into comes from different sources. It might arise from the external environment via interaction with teammates. It can also come from within by means of our kinesthetic consciousness—that is, the sensations by which we perceive body position, weight, muscle tension, and movement. Athletes who are connected to the feedback given by their bodies and movements are able to stay connected and in control. Awareness of the quality of your ideal performance state is a skill that gives you instant feedback and thus allows you to create the right movement. It is here that you can make the adjustments needed to maintain or return to your optimum level. As we'll see, it is through training and repetition that your brain will learn to filter information and thus keep you from being overwhelmed.

CONCENTRATION

One of the foundations for the Zone is concentration. We're able to stay focused on the present by concentrating on action and ignoring what has previously happened, our worries, and/or our future expectations. In the Zone champions talk about being focused on what they do, on their movements and feelings. This total immersion in the present is what golfer Tony Jacklin has described as a "cocoon of concentration."

But concentrating on a task does not necessarily mean that you stay focused throughout an entire performance. It's important to know how to stop and then quickly refocus. Similarly, hearing the crowd may indicate not a lack of concentration but rather a unified immersion that includes the crowd.

CONTROL

Tom Kite, one of the best golfers of the early 1990s, says of the Zone, "When it happens you are in total control. Nothing bothers you." This feeling derives, in part, from the fact that you trust your skills and know the task is feasible. The result is a sense of power, confidence, and calm. This control frees the athlete from the fear of failure. Former NBA player Byron Scott says it well: "All you can hear is this little voice inside you, telling you 'shoot' every time you touch the ball. Because you know it's going in." Or Chris Evert: "You can't miss anything. It's like you anticipate, way ahead of time, earlier than usual, where the ball is going and you also know where you're going to hit the ball before you hit."

LOSS OF SELF-CONSCIOUSNESS

Control helps us put aside doubt and fatigue, lose our self-consciousness, and thus simply have fun in our sport. The loss of self-consciousness in the heart of the action is actually a powerful feature because in the Zone, our perception of ourselves is really more confident, strong, and positive.

TIME DISTORTION

Perhaps the most bizarre aspect of the Zone is its transformation of the notions of space and, most often, time. In the heat of the game, time can seem to accelerate; or it might slow down and stretch indefinitely, giving the perception that we have all the time in the world. Chris Evert recalls, "Everything seems slower, so you have more time to adjust." Bill Walton: "Everything slows down. It's like everybody is wearing cement shoes, the ball is in slow motion, everything slows down except you, and you feel like you're operating at a different speed and at a different level than anybody else."

In this modified state of consciousness, sometimes the athlete perceives a suspension of time, as related by Roger Bannister after his world-record mile: "I felt that the moment of a lifetime had come. There was no pain, only a great unity of movement and aim. The world seemed to stand still, or did not exist. The only reality was the next two hundred yards of track under my feet. The tape meant finality—extinction perhaps."

Finally, Johnny Miller, winner of over twenty titles on the golf pro tour, gives us the definition of another dimension: "I think the Zone is really being in harmony with what you're doing. Wanting to do it, wanting to do it for the right reasons, not for money or for greed or for power. That doesn't get you in the Zone." This dimension can only be reached if we're engaged in an experience that is rewarding in itself, not by what it can possibly give us (earnings, trophies, fame).

All these components have been described, especially in the bestseller *Flow in Sports*[6] by Jackson and Czikszentmihalyi, as well as "How to Reach Your Sports Zone" by psychologists Annemarie Infantino Murphy and Shane Murphy.[8] Other sports psychologists have added other essential components to our understanding.

More Factors That Contribute to the Zone Experience

IMAGINATION

Most important is the ability to think creatively—that is, to use our imagination through mental imagery and sensations.

POSITIVE THOUGHTS

Positive thinking helps us stay confident. We all have a small voice within us. If it speaks in a negative way, we perform poorly. Positive thinking changes our internal dialogue and directs the mind in a constructive manner.

HIGH ENERGY

Many athletes describe a feeling of great energy during a

BACK TO THE ZONE

performance. This ability to mobilize energy allows us to continue even when fatigue is present.

SELF-ESTEEM

Golf coach Gail Smirthwaite describes another important and often overlooked component of the Zone: self-esteem. Indeed, "low self-esteem will make it almost impossible for someone to be able to create the 'flow state' on demand, because they do not have the 'belief' that they can achieve the success they seek and often their minds are full of negativity at the point they should be in the 'flow state.'"

EASE

In the Zone, as athletes often report, body and mind operate at their limits with little effort. The phenomenon is well summarized by Daniel Goleman: "In the flow state the hardest things are easy, making the exceptional performance completely natural."[9]

ALTERED STATE OF CONSCIOUSNESS

An interesting Zone feature that is not yet well understood has been identified by Christine Le Scanff, professor of sports psychology in France. In her book *Modified Consciousness*,[10] she describes a certain amnesia that makes it difficult or even impossible to describe a Zone performance. Bob Trumpy, a former football player, gives us a good example: "It was like being in a tunnel and being blinded by a bright light. When I came out of the other end of the tunnel, I was in the end zone and my teammates were celebrating. To this day I still don't remember what I did."

Le Scanff notes a detachment that gives an athlete increased tolerance to pain while he or she experiences no fatigue, boredom, or exhaustion: "Sport would also allow [an athlete] to achieve an altered state of consciousness—in a physiological way because of the secretion by the body's own biological drugs: endorphins, enkephalin, adrenaline. Beta-endorphin has analgesic power fifty times higher than that of morphine. [It's] a metabolic secretion certainly linked to the enjoyment experienced by the athlete, which urges him to repeat very difficult efforts to go beyond a certain pain threshold."

Thus the effects of both mental and emotional fatigue can be reduced by training under conditions of fatigue. Strategies to maintain intensity and focus when we are tired give us the tools we need when the body tells the mind to stop but the mind asks the body to continue.

Remember your feelings and
your sensations.
What are your optimal conditions?

Focus on the process.
Have clear goals and write them down.

Be aware of feedback.
The first source is your body!

Focus on what really matters.
Control only what you can.

See your sport differently: Think creatively.
What do you create?

Use positive affirmations.

Be proud of all the hard work
you have done.

Note the ease you feel.
Feel the energy.

Now you won't be surprised when
you reach the Zone!

I set clear and simple goals for myself.

The dark side of the Zone

Where your mind goes, everything follows.
—Terry Orlick

For all its benefit, the Zone features a detachment from pain that can have a downside. A point never previously addressed Zone studies is the existence of a "bad" Zone, a Zone that can lead us beyond our limits, to our detriment. Dr. John Douillard emphasizes "the existence of two different experiences of the Zone. One is born of integration and harmony between mind and body, the other from a breakdown between the two."[11] This can occur, for example, after or during endurance events. The Tour du Mont Blanc in France or the Western States 100 Mile Endurance Run in the United States are known to produce such experiences.

After enduring dozens of miles in the heat or the night, followed by rock climbing at high altitude, the body reaches its limits. The mind, however, remains intent on its goal: to finish the race, whatever the cost. The runner feels great, she feels at the top, but in reality her performance completely breaks down. John Douillard tells of one runner competing in the Western States 100 Mile Endurance Run: "Exhausted and delirious, he had collapsed and couldn't take another step, yet he said he had been feeling 'fantastic' until his legs gave out and he collapsed." This raises the question: How did he go from feeling so good to so bad, so fast? Douillard answers: "Painkilling endorphins gave him a false sense of euphoria, which masked the body's extreme fatigue. Because his mind was disconnected from his body, he could not muster the simple coordination needed to stand up and walk." He adds: "When exhaustion occurs and the body is in pain—severe overheating; painful knees, ankles, and shins; aching lungs; and so on—the body begins to produce painkillers to help the person endure the ordeal. These painkillers, in the form of endorphins, enkephalons, and other morphine-like substances, are generated to combat the physical punishment inflicted on the body by a mind that is out of touch with what is happening on the physical level. The runner feels high, but his performance is disintegrated. As the flood of endorphins is released into the bloodstream, it does more than kill the pain; as the mind swims in the pool of morphine, it becomes numb to the body."

Though at first glance, it is easy to assume that this runner was in the Zone, this is not the legitimate Zone athletes seek. The true Zone does not segregate the body and mind; rather, they are inseparable, synergized together without effort.

Ask yourself: Was it really the Zone or simply another great performance?

Learn to better listen to your body.

Take the time to read
Body, Mind, and Sport by John Douillard.

I pay attention to how my body is feeling.

The fake Zone

Is the Zone real or fake? If we consider the reports of athletes and coaches on this question, we must look more closely at a study on basketball by Thomas Gilovich from Cornell and his colleagues Robert Vallone and Amos Tversky from Stanford.[12] They suggest that sometimes it is possible for athletes to incorrectly report having been in the Zone simply because they experienced more intense feelings and sensations. This hypothesis naturally makes some people ask whether the Zone is real (a different perceptual and cognitive state acting positively on performance), or if it is just something that athletes report to explain their high performance.

The Zone is more than your best performance.

Measuring the Zone?

From the above parameters, some people have sought to measure the Zone with scientific tools. In 1996 Susan Jackson developed the Flow State Scale, a questionnaire designed to measure it. More recently, Dr. Julia Schueler, a psychologist at the University of Zurich, has attempted to quantify the harmony between body and mind that seems present in the flow state. In a study with marathon runners, her team showed that the subjective experience of flow and the hormone cortisol varied jointly, suggesting interdependency between the state of flow and the body.

However, Csikszentmihalyi warns of the dangers of any measure of flow: "When we said the flow is defined as a score in the flow questionnaire, we lost it. The concept of flow describes a complex psychological state that has significant consequences on human life. Any measures of flow that we create are only a partial reflection of this reality." The flow cannot be captured by numbers, sampling methods, or interviews. Yes, we are always looking to press our tools of analysis and measurement of phenomena. But *the Zone is not just chemical, or just kinetic, or just mental—it is all of these at once.*

In dissecting something that is global in nature, we run into a wall because, admittedly, our scientific tools are not yet adapted to this inner experience. We cannot measure everything. Do we measure happiness or joy?

> **We don't need to measure the Zone!**

Flow or Zone?

Open yourself and flow at once with the total flowing now.
—Bruce Lee

According to Julia Schueler, harmony between body and mind is not enough to achieve flow. In her flow experiments the body is not as involved—they feature, for instance, chess, video games, or reading. "Maybe the flow in sport is not the same as the flow in intellectual tasks? Perhaps a distinction is necessary?" This question is not yet fully answered but actually points to another key issue in the study of the Zone.

Studies often refer to flow or the Zone without really distinguishing the difference between the two, generating confusion. Although Dr. Janet Young,[13] a sports psychologist and former professional tennis player, does not distinguish between flow and Zone, in contrast a study conducted by Susan Jackson suggests that flow is the process, whereas the Zone is the ultimate experience.

I like to think of it this way: The flow is the path by which we can access the Zone, which in turn is much more than the sum of its parts.

See the flow as the process.
See the Zone as the ultimate experience.

Zone at will!

Keith Henschen, a sports psychologist at the University of Utah–Salt Lake City, argues that the experience of the Zone can be cultivated intentionally. He is joining Csikszentmiha-lyi, who sees the flow as an experience that may result from our own efforts: If the right conditions are present, then flow occurs. However, other sports psychologists—including Bob Rotella, who works with pro golfers—don't share this opinion: "It happens when it happens, and thinking about it just gets in the way of it happening at all. Self-transcendence, a characteristic of the zone at its most profound, cannot be produced by force of will." For psychologist Abraham Maslow, peak experiences are spontaneous events; there is no connection between our actions and the experience itself. This leads some psychologists to question whether there is any sense of trying to enter the Zone!

The Zone is not a question of will.

Forget any idea of control.

I relax and focus only on what I can control.

Optimal conditions

With one eye you are looking at the outside world, while with the other you are looking within yourself.
—Amedeo Modigliani

We can work on developing each individual characteristic of the Zone with the proven techniques. But we often stop at this point: *Here are the ingredients. Now it's up to you to play!* How do we best combine these ingredients in order to reach the Zone? Must we independently work each component? Is there an order? Johnny Miller sums up the problem: "The zone is the most elusive thing in sports, maybe one of the most exclusive clubs in the world. I think it's a lot like a complex recipe for a dish or a pie and if you miss one ingredient, it doesn't taste quite right. In golf there's a recipe to get into the zone." So let's see how to access the "Zone cuisine."

For some athletes at the top of their art, the Zone occurs so often that it seems perfectly natural (think of Roger Federer or Rafael Nadal). For most athletes, however, the quest to reach the Zone comes from doing the hard work of re-creating and maintaining the experience.

In United States and the UK, the last twenty years have seen a proliferation of books and articles offering advice on how to achieve the Zone in tennis, basketball, golf, and other sports. Although the quality of such publications varies greatly, their popularity attests to the vast public interest in this subject.

So we have a plethora of information at our disposal: athletes' experiences, coaches' observations, theories and advice from sports psychologists, and observations from neuroscience. Each gives us detailed information about our brain in a Zone state (we will dwell on this further in part 2). If we disregard some clinicians for whom the prerequisite to entering the Zone is long-term psychotherapy during which the athletes work through conflicts related to their performance, we have at our disposal many tips and techniques that aim to further establish the components of the Zone.

For Jim Taylor, a sports psychologist in the United States, the Zone is an ephemeral experience. His goal is consistently high levels of performance under difficult conditions—that is, being able to stay in the flow state as long as possible. "I emphasize a consistently high level of performance under the most challenging conditions. If athletes can achieve that, then they will perform well consistently . . . What makes the great ones great is not the occasional amazing performances, but rather consistently high level performances across a season or career." He therefore focuses on bringing together all elements of performance, whether cognitive, emotional, physical, technical, or tactical; the optimal performance state can only be achieved with all these factors together. He gives a simple image to illustrate this idea: "Flow can't be achieved with conscious effort. It is like sleep; you can't try to sleep. All you can do is create the conditions in which sleep will come." He adds: "Then, periodically, all will fall together and flow will occur for those truly transcendental performances."

Costas Karageorghis, a doctor of sports psychology at Brunel University (UK), gives us some guidelines for entering the Zone. Among them is "anchoring," an attention control technique that helps calm an athlete and allows him to be focused during critical moments. Anchoring involves awareness and control of breath and posture. It is typically used in sports where there are many breaks, such as volleyball or tennis, and can also be useful in alpine skiing.

We can of course find help by developing our mental imagery. Imagery can be used before and during the performance, like some sprinters who internally run a perfect race before they enter the starting blocks. *The secret to high-quality imagery is using all your senses used to create an image as vivid and real as possible.* Encourage the effective combination of your senses by immersing yourself in sport sequences, closing your eyes and noting the colors, shapes, and textures. You can also embed images of success by creating a mental picture of success—a vision that meets your goals and dreams, and that you can refer to enhance your mental image.

Another technique to access the Zone is the use of both positive statements and keywords that reinforce what you are trying to do. Many golfers use such words as *fluid, relax,* and so on. Athletes can find a word that symbolizes what they are attempting to do and use it at critical moments to induce a state of complete concentration or relaxation. These keywords can also be triggers of the process leading to the Zone.

This is the approach of Jim Loehr, a leading US sports psychologist who has worked with champions such as Jim Courier and Martina Navratilova. His focus is primarily on the cultivation of a positive mind-set in competition. What happens in the mind has direct effects on the body—and vice versa, because negative reactions can sabotage performance This negative cycle is self-reinforcing: Anxiety and fear affect physiology, resulting in a bad performance, which in turn perpetuates more anxiety and fear. Negative thoughts can have devastating consequences both psychologically and physically.

Conversely, it is also possible to consciously cultivate a cycle of positive reinforcement: Positive thoughts lead to feelings of enthusiasm and determination. Jim Loehr says, "An athlete's thoughts prompt certain emotions, and those emotions have psychological consequences. Thoughts about losing, for example, may lead to fear and anxiety. In turn, those feelings prompt an array of physiological responses including increased heart rate, muscle tightness, shortness of breath, reduced blood flow to the hands and feet, and even narrowing of vision." What is interesting here is that *the body can also trigger a positive cycle. Techniques based on posture and breathing can help loosen us and lead to a more positive attitude.*

Positive affirmations and keywords can also find their place in a routine of self-hypnosis. This can be an effective way to take control of yourself so that you don't depend on competition to reach the Zone. This technique allows the activation of the more creative right hemisphere of the brain and limits the conscious mental activity of the left hemisphere. Thus self-hypnosis can have a positive effect against anxiety and negative self-talk. Once mastered, self-hypnosis can very quickly bring calm and relaxation. It simply involves focusing your attention on a single thought. For example, you can focus on the regularity of your breathing. This is what makes Czikszentmihalyi says that flow is a "semi-hypnotic" state. Another way to achieve a hypnotic state is the repetition of keywords such as *relax* or *easy*. Gary Mack, an expert in sport hypnosis, emphasizes the similarities between people in a hypnotic state and those who are in the Zone, especially concerning the distortion of time.

All these routines or rituals are not mere superstition. They can be seen as a method of conditioning that promotes concentration and enhances feelings of control and confidence—but whose hidden purpose is to help us switch to another state of consciousness. In his book *The Mind of Champions,*[14] Hubert Ripoll, a professor of sports science at the University of the Mediterranean, gives us a key to the alchemy that helps direct the emergence of the Zone. According to him, we must first try to place ourselves in circumstances similar to those that have conducted the Zone before; in short: to create a favorable environment.

Here the routines and cues that trigger a shift of consciousness can be best utilized. Here Ripoll introduces an important concept used in psychology: the boot. According to this concept, those of us who have had an experience of the Zone can reenter it via our memories of it, which in fact left a strong imprint in our nervous system.

We can also trigger the process that will bring together all the components of the Zone created by routines, which should lead to a different state of consciousness. This boot is always something simple like a word or a movement. Hubert Ripoll identifies three phases of boot: "The first about a month before the start of the competition, designed to pro-

duce a background level, through which the mind is optimally configured, followed by a second phase . . . engaged on
the day of the event, which brings the mind under tension
until the beginning of it. A third phase occurs about three to
five minutes before the event. This phase is very specific,
because the athlete must then go into a 'bubble' that should
not be completely hermetic, and must filter the information
necessary to the sport." Then comes the performance, when
the athlete experiences all the sensations described above.
This gradual Zone-building process is supported by the testimonies of champions who felt they were entering the Zone
at different times (in the locker room, several days or weeks
beforehand, or the like). This reinforces the idea that made
us initially differentiate between the state of flow (the process
of setting up all the ingredients) and the Zone (which is limited in time and with a higher intensity).

Many believe that champions have never learned the
process leading to the Zone, discovering this state intuitively
without being guided and without training. Is this true?
When we learn a little more about our great champions, we

often find that there was a learning phase in all their successful routines. We can even talk about conditioning. A good example is that of former number one tennis player Ivan Lendl. Jim Loehr traveled with Lendl in 1990. At that time he was in his fourth consecutive number one year: "Between matches, he spent long hours on the court grooving his strokes, and he adopted a fierce physical conditioning regimen. But he also spent nearly as much time training control of his mind. He regularly practiced observing his thoughts and emotions the way that a meditator might, for example, simply noting their arising and passing without reacting to them. He also did mental-focus exercises in order to strengthen the sharpness of his awareness and his capacity to be absorbed in one thing at a time. Before matches, he sat down and briefly reviewed his goals—'Be strong, confident, eager, quick,' he might write—in order to program his mind more positively. Finally, he closed his eyes and imagined himself executing the goals on the court—sometimes taking himself through entire games."

This process is clearly the result more of disciplined and balanced training than of innate qualities!

During tough moments, remember:
awareness, breath control, and posture.

Watch the pros.

Learn to recognize your optimal environment.

When you visualize: associate feelings,
sensations, colors, smells, scenes, shapes.

Your body and breath can help you
to get back on the positive path.

Create your personal routine. You know
better than anyone what feels right for you.

Choose two positive words to trigger your Zone.

Don't overrate talent! No matter what skills you
were born with, you can always create your
ideal conditions.

I always believe in my ability to do well.

Zone for everybody?

Being in the zone does not require technical expertise. I've seen beginners there, not thinking, just focused, and doing what their bodies at their level are capable of.

—Tim Gallwey

A major controversy in the study of the Zone is whether it is accessible to everyone or limited to a small number of super-champions. Some believe that the Zone is the reward for hard work and preparation. For Richard Schonborn, a former national technical director in Germany during the period that saw the emergence of Steffi Graf and Boris Becker, it is something very individual and personal. He believes it depends on many factors: age, talent, technique, frequency of training, but above all the level of expertise achieved by the athlete. He refers to a study revealing that it takes about ten years and ten thousand hours of training to reach a technically elite level. However, he adds that even before acquiring this level of expertise, we can still reach this state during a match or training, but often this situation will not last.

This may indicate that expertise is more a question of maintaining the Zone through awareness of our body and feelings. Sports psychologist Keith Henschen doesn't think anyone can achieve this state easily. The goal of his interventions with athletes is to help them to reach the Zone more often.

From the perspective of information processing, *expert* refers to one who enjoys optimum treatment of information. So if you are just starting to learn something, your brain will be processing action very differently from the way it'll work once you've mastered the technique. The assumption is that when we start, the conscious process takes over and prevents us from reaching the Zone. That's why Hubert Ripoll say: "The first encounter with this state happens only after many years of practice, when certain conditions are met as intense pressure caused by an exceptional challenge and thorough preparation."

Do we really need to achieve a level of fully automated movements to experience the Zone? Can beginners and amateurs not enjoy this experience? This is not the opinion of Dr. John Douillard: "This 'exercise high,' in which dynamical physical activity coexists with the inner experience of composure and calm, is not exclusive to athletes; it can be reached by anyone, regardless of his or her level of fitness. Our preliminary studies indicate that anyone can experience the Zone or 'runner's high' at will." This is a view shared by Tim Gallwey, author of *The Inner Game of Tennis,* who believes that the inner experiences of the Zone are accessible to everybody. Indeed, in many studies Zone experiences occur for adults who have spent years working their athletic skills, but as Mike Murphy has shown in his work,[15] *extraordinary experiences in sports can occur in youths and even among those who are not "natural" athletes.*

We can also wonder whether the Zone in sport is similar in feeling and intensity to its appearance in other activities such as music or art. Some speculate that when the body is involved, the experience is different in nature. However, interviews with musicians and other artists show that they describe the same sensations and feelings as athletes. I believe it is more a universal experience.

You don't need to wait ten thousand hours
to reach the Zone!

Pay attention to the signs
announcing your Zone.

Learn from your life experiences
and use them in your sport.

*I am open and receptive to the
abundant energy the Universe offers.*

*I have the ability to express
and expand my Zone.*

Inner sun

Music in the soul can be heard by the universe.

—Lao-tsu

"It's deeper, it's an emotion. It cannot be said with words why you love, it does not pass through the mind. It puts me in a certain state of receptivity, of sensibility. I called this state, state of inspiration, which is not a normal state. The state of love is not a normal state. There is something that touches you deep down, that certainly puts you in touch with what there is inside you of the truest, of the purest . . . Why is it revealed? This reveals a pure part of ourselves, a beautiful part. It touches something deep . . . and we think it's beautiful. It puts us in touch with our inner beauty, truth, something where there is no mask, there is no game, there is nothing left . . . a sort of inner sun.

Reading these words, you might believe they are the testimony of an Olympic champion. They're not! These are the words of French musician Michel Jonasz[16] describing his feelings while listening to Bach. He also spoke of the Zone, connecting with something bigger. The similarity with testimonies of athletes is striking. You can find similar stories in the pioneering work of Mike Murphy and his friends in the late 1970s; these studies paved the way to seeing sports as an area of human transcendence.

Music is another way to reach the Zone.
As you feel the music, feel your sport.

What do you feel when you listen your favorite music?

Remember this great energy.
Remember your Inner Sun.
It's always available to you.

I close my eyes and listen to my favorite music.
As I breathe, I feel the energy of the music.

What prevents us from reaching the Zone?

We tend to overanalyze a lot of things in this sport.

—Pete Sampras

Many obstacles can prevent us from touching the Zone, among them overanalysis and judgment. Some athletes report that they become distracted by the presence of spectators, judges, or other competitors. The anxiety caused by observers is a natural fear associated with any judgment of value. Learning to lose self-consciousness is therefore a key parameter for entering the Zone.

Peter Spang, a former professional player and tennis coach, puts forward four other obstacles: *perfectionism, self-criticism, boredom,* and *expectations.* Here I add three more challenges on the road to the Zone: *fear, fatigue,* and *lack of flexibility.* Indeed, the main obstacle that prevents us from being in the moment is fear.

During the performance, we must also deal with fatigue.

> **"We cannot be fully present when we are afraid. That's what keeps us from really letting go."**
> **—Author**

How can we stay in the Zone when the body begins to function differently? How can an athlete handle this problem? Dr. Virginie Van Wassenhove, director of a brain imaging center in Paris, says: "The less focused you are on your self (as experiencing pain, fatigue, etc.), the less intense [these feelings] will be. Alternatively you could teach your brain to consider a certain type of pain as leading to a pleasurable feeling as opposed to a painful one. That's a mystery. Focusing on the future, not the present, may do the trick also." This echoes the findings of a recent study of biathletes showing that we can overcome fatigue and pain by directing our attention not to our body and our feelings, but toward an external point.

Finally, a pitfall to avoid is seeking to experience the exact same sensations as before. Even if the feeling of victory is important, trying to re-create exactly the same feelings as your first Zone is unrealistic. Of course some parameters stay the same, but what makes the Zone so elusive is its flexibility and this can be the hardest aspect to work and control. As outlined in "Optimal Conditions," creating favorable conditions and initiating the memory of our first Zone experience can have positive effects, but expecting the exact same sensations can increase rigidity and thus form an obstacle to the Zone.

Don't judge yourself.

Be aware of your fears.

Stay fit to avoid early fatigue.

Don't stay stuck in the past.
Don't try to feel the same.
Everything changes.

Let yourself be absorbed by the present.

---

*When I stay positive and focused,
everything is possible.*

Now what?

Do whatever you feel like—do what you love. Whatever you do, do it well.

—Arthur Ashe

This overview of the Zone allows us to see that for most of us, it is an unusual state resulting from a delicate balance of ingredients brought together by an alchemy that still eludes us. We must recognize that when touching on questions related to consciousness, we are still a bit helpless. And the first obstacles to our understanding are often our language and culture. We feel that the Zone is more than the sum of technical, physiological, or psychological states—but what is the link among them? Should we turn to pleasure and passion? Because one thing is certain: *All the champions who have touched the Zone were guided by one thing in common—passion and love of their sport.*

The link to the Zone lies in your passion.

This energy, this light that you first saw and felt as a kid, is always here for you.

I'm doing something I love to do.

Part Two

The Zone is within

Have fun—Life is a sport—Play, and the Zone will be yours.
—Mike Lardon

Limits

At the end of what you must know,
You are only at the beginning of what you must feel.
—Kahlil Gibran

Life is too deep for words, so don't try to describe it, just live it.
—C. S. Lewis

For some athletes, performance in the Zone is reached only few minutes into their careers and yet it will mark them for life. What makes this experience so special? In the first part of this book, we saw that coaches, athletes, and executives dream of putting the Zone in a box, finding its formula or breaking its mystery. But this is not something that can be bought on the Internet! A visit to a bookstore shows us that many claim to have found the answer. Some give us seven, others eight, nine, or ten fundamentals to entering the Zone. The problem is, none of this works at all!

The descriptions and efforts of specialists in sport and psychology should not hide our limited understanding the phenomenon. Because can we really get into the Zone using all the techniques science and psychology have given to us? It is indeed a paradox here: To enter the Zone we need to stop overanalyzing, but the techniques supposed to help us bring even more . . . technical analysis!

The approach used in the early stages of learning—breaking a subject down into parts and learning everything separately before putting together again—does not apply to the Zone because this goes against one of the main components: instinctive action.

The problem is that if sports psychology allows us to identify the Zone's essential characteristics, it is still young and shows the limits of our current tools for studying subjective experiences. Ken Ravizza, a professor of psychology at California State University who wrote for years on what he calls "peak experiences," also criticizes the lack of interest in the subjective experience of the athlete.

Here we are going beyond the description of features by looking at how to live these special moments. There is indeed a missing piece in the puzzle. Something that still eludes us.

Let's continue our quest for the Zone at the gates of consciousness—the limits of knowledge and science.

Go beyond your technique.

What prevents you from being in the Zone?

What is your missing piece?

To resume your quest to the Zone:
Know who you are.

There is something inside me that is greater than any obstacle.

Neurosciences

The biology of mind bridges the sciences—concerned with the natural world—and the humanities—concerned with the meaning of human experience. Insights that come from this new synthesis will lead to a deeper understanding of ourselves.

—Eric R. Kandel, winner of the Nobel Prize for Medicine

To better grasp the Zone we can first look at neuroscience. Not to measure it, but rather to indirectly see the changes in our body, particularly the activity of the brain. New brain imaging technologies are a vital way to update our understanding of the neurophysiological mechanisms involved in the state of the Zone. We know in particular that the presence of beta waves is the signature of an active athlete. You would then expect the athlete in a beta state to be in a better place to compete. But in fact—not really. Research has shown that just before reaching a peak of performance, the brain is producing *alpha* waves, especially the left side, already identified in states of inner calm and relaxation.

In this state, the synchronization between the centers of the brain improves, allowing better processing of information. A popular idea therefore is that those who can shift from the beta state (active) to the alpha state (relaxed but still alert) will be able to break away from mechanical performance and thus reach the Zone.

This condition can be reproduced in particular through the imprint created by the emotional charge associated with our initial experience of the Zone. The neuronal connections created during each experience are in fact always associated with our emotions. And in the Zone they are positive emotions. So the more we live these experiences, the more we will have a chance to live them again.

The Zone also features more efficient functioning of the brain that requires less energy. Daniel Goleman,[17] an advocate of emotional intelligence, notes that while in a state of flow the hardest things are easy; outstanding performances seem quite natural. Inside the brain, there is a similar paradox: The most complicated tasks are accomplished with a minimum expenditure of energy. In the Zone, an athlete's brain shifts into a mode of optimum energy consumption, translated into a passage into automatic mode. Hubert Ripoll sheds light on this in his book *The Mind of Champions:* "The essence of automation is to be activated quickly and without significant cognitive effort, and [athletes] say that their activation is low"—the opposite of high-level, complex operations that consume a lot of mental energy.[18] For Ripoll the Zone is simply a much better use of information processing systems, which often leads him to compare champions to computers!

**Your emotions are a great source of energy.
Learn how to tap into them.**

**Don't hide your emotions. Acknowledge them
and keep the positive ones only.**

---

*My emotions are a dynamic
and creative power.*

Modified perceptions

Every second is of infinite value.

—Johann Wolfgang von Goethe

Changes in the brain may be one cause of the modified perceptions reported by champions: a different perception of time, a better vision, more vivid sensations, but also a modification of their state of consciousness. What psychologists call altered or modified states of consciousness are controlled by a neural structure that regulates an individual's level of vigilance and filters messages from the senses and from outside. This level of alertness is controlled by hormones that may play a key role in the state of the Zone. This is the explanation of Christine Le Scanff, a professor of sports psychology at the Université Paris–Sud: "Sport would allow [one] to achieve an altered state of consciousness, and this organically because of . . . the body's own biological drugs: endorphin, enkephalin, epinephrine, substances linked to increased vigilance, which could explain the bursts of hyper-consciousness of athletes."[19] Amazingly, she makes a clear distinction, as Hubert Ripoll does, between on the one hand the states experienced during spiritual practices or practices such as yoga or meditation, and on the other the Zone experienced in sport. Spiritual practices cut the person off from the world, while the athlete must instead enter a state of intense physical presence that creates the best movement.

Maybe people jump to conclusions too quickly and in particular ignore hundreds of testimonials from athletes gathered in the late 1970s by George Leonard and Michael Murphy at the Esalen Sports Center in California showing the similarity of these states of consciousness in sports and in other areas such as art or music.

Athletes also report that in the Zone, their vision is no longer the same. For example, the golfer Payne Stewart has said: "When it's happens, all you see is the ball and the hole." Or Bill Walton: "You don't see the crowd. Really all you can see is the boundary of the court. You can't see the players on the bench. You can see the coach but not the guys on the bench. You don't see the crowd, but you know they're there. It's just a big fog." Christy Frikken, professional skydiver: "How vision relates to performance and flow is a particularly interesting question in regards to competitive skydiving. In 4-way skydiving the physical demands are not as great as the decision-making process and precision. In skydiving vision can be a key indicator of whether a person has the right arousal level. As arousal gets too high, vision tends to narrow and almost becomes a dark cone. Athletes stop seeing important details or over-focusing on the incorrect cues when they are over this line. When you are 'on the line' you have enough physiological arousal to increase your physical performance, but not enough to impair that decision-making process. In this stage your vision feels clearer, brighter, and wider. At the same time irrelevant details are easily ignored and discarded."

Did you ever notice a change in your perceptions?

Next time during your warm-up, be aware of what you feel, see, and hear.

I breathe deeply.
I feel how my lungs expand.
I feel how my vision expands.

To shift our attention

I shut my eyes in order to see.
—Paul Gauguin

There is more to vision than meets the eyes.
—Jacob Liberman

If the Zone is a matter of perception, perhaps we can play with our senses to try to enter it. In particular, we have seen that the athletes living the Zone are experiencing a change in vision. We also know that the athlete in the Zone is focused on the task at hand while keeping a great awareness of what is happening around him. A logical question is: Can we play on our vision and thus control our attention in order to enter the Zone and stay there as long as possible?

We know that the best athletes, via their knowledge of the visual patterns and tactics of their sport, have the ability to pick up the right clues and also to anticipate precise trajectories and actions. But our vision has other hidden features. A clue is given by Mihaly Csikszentmihalyi, who stresses the importance of vision in the development of flow: "Vision can be more than the detection of information. The advantage over a lot of techniques or activities is that seeing is immediately accessible!"

We also know that in stressful situations our vision is affected: Our focus grows narrower. That's what makes John Gorrie, author of *Performing in the Zone,* say: "You can see the level of an athlete's performance by looking at his eyes."[20] We must therefore look at our attention, as suggested by Christy Frikken: "When performing in the zone, we move forward focusing on the next move and allow our subconscious to alert us to exceptions. We might see some subtle cue about our teammate's body position or facial expression with a glimpse in just a fraction of a fraction of a moment. I can't intentionally look for this sign, but if I am in the zone I see it and it is translated into a feeling, which in turn guides an instant decision to hesitate appropriately before continuing. I don't know if you could train your vision to enter the zone. I don't think it is a challenge of vision, I think it is a challenge of shifting attention."

Probably the first to have understood the importance of this shift of attention is Scott Ford,[21] a tennis teacher in Denver, Colorado. For thirty years he has studied the relationship between the Zone and attention. With the help of Bill Hines, an ophthalmologist specializing in sport vision, and Michael Meshes, a neuroscientist, he has developed a method of tennis training based on a shift in attention. His hypothesis: A shift of focus allows a complete shift of consciousness, and thus helps us enter the Zone more often. This method simply uses the fact that by shifting our attention we call to another part of our brain, one that can more quickly process information because it's more instinctive. Geoff Mangum, a golf coach passionate about neuroscience, explains this mechanism: "There are two visual pathways in the brain's neural networks: once for identifying static information about objects, and another one for action in relation to objects and locations in space (the so-called 'what' and 'where' systems). In sports, there is no 'what' worth noticing. In golf specifically, and in putting more specifically, 'it's a hole—they're all alike' and 'it's a ball—they're all alike.'" The system "where" uses brain mechanisms that use less energy, which we have seen correspond to the areas related to automation. Basically, this means: Be alert to the "where" and the body will take care of it! Thus, Ford and Mangum naturally teach to first focus our attention on the ball and the contact, then change the visual mode with a look at the contact area. I have also shown that this shift of attention could be extended even farther by keeping the gaze a little longer on this contact zone, with a sort of dead gaze or soft eyes.[22]

That's exactly what is observed with Roger Federer or Rafael Nadal. These champions do not seem to watch the ball after contact; they remain focused just a little longer on the contact area. Their attention is not fixed but shifts from close attention on the ball to larger attention to the contact zone. Scientists call this skill attentional flexibility. This does not mean that Federer is not focused when he plays; only that he has the ability to switch his attention to what really matters. It's a sort of super-consciousness in which "you focus on nothing but see everything." Fiona Taylor, six-time world champion in windsurfing, calls this type of gaze "soft eyes" and says: "When we 'soften our gaze' and go into an expanded state of consciousness we are able to have focus of the internal and external without having to think."

This gaze also appears in the advice given by Kazumi

Tabata, a great master of Shokotan Karate, who presents in his book *Secret Tactics* some essential aspects of martial arts: "Seeing without seeing. It is crucial not to fix your eyes at a specific location." He explains why: "The important thing is not to stop the mind on anything. This is an essential point. If you stop the mind, it will be captured by your opponent. If you move with the intention to be quick, your mind will be caught by your own intention. If you direct the mind toward something outside of yourself, it will be captured by its destination and you will be defeated. Then where should you put the mind? This is my answer: you must not put the mind anywhere. Then it will expand out to fill the entire body. If the mind is not put in one place, it is everywhere."[23]

In our example, tennis, vision is used to collect the right information; then the visual system shifts, entering into a kind of rest mode and allowing instinctive action. If your attention is focused on following the trajectory of the ball, for example, your response will never be a perfect movement. On the contrary, champions assign less energy to the visual system, and the excess energy can be used for movement. In a way, to do less is to do better!

This process helps to simplify the chain of information and allows us to move faster. Indeed, we know that what we look at is intimately connected to our sensory channels (auditory, visual, or kinesthetic). This process is obviously unconscious. Thus, the movement of our eyes provides access to the mechanisms of thought. For example, an eye movement to the top right usually means we are remembering images.

And what interests us here is that a look downward and to the left means that we are in a kinesthetic mode. We feel our body sensations and emotions. This is precisely what champions do better than others. In this case, vision is no longer used only to take in information but also to switch from a visual mode to a proprioceptive mode. Champions have the ability to direct their gaze in order to place themselves naturally in the kinesthetic channel! Their recipe is simple: The more you play, the more you create the conditions of the Zone, and more likely you are to stay there! Because throughout the game, you do not need to think about complicated things. You just have to do the simplest thing: hit the ball.

Until recently, nobody was really aware of the role of vision in the Zone state. Now, with the work of the team of

Scott Ford and my work on the role of soft eyes, we know that by learning to use our vision differently and adopting the right attention, we can create favorable conditions for a leap of consciousness and thus perhaps the onset of the Zone.

Trust your vision. You already know where and what to watch.

During your movement, soften your gaze. Don't try to focus on something; only focus on what you feel.

Trust your senses.

Don't try to understand what happens. Just do it.

As I walk, I breathe deeply.
I slow down and notice
how my attention widens.

A gold vision

Perception is continuous awareness.
—Bruce Lee

The eye is the lamp of the body.
If your eye is sound, your whole body will be full of light.
—Jesus

Some exceptional athletes, during or after their careers, have examined their experience of the Zone. Because if the Zone seems mysterious to many, it seems that some meet the Zone more often. Drew Ginn, three-time Olympic rowing champion (1994, 1996, and 2000), describes moments when for him, "The past and the future are fading and reality becomes clear." He demonstrates the importance of vision, sensation, and intuition. Ginn's first advice is to help us get closer to the Zone: "During training or competition, it is really important to listen to feelings. When I open these messages that are accessible to all of us, I found a great ease but also a great efficiency. You better move when you're aware of your body. You feel better when you're aware of your mind. And you see better when you realize your vision. Similarly, many athletes show a different vision in the Zone." Ginn adds: "Being in the moment is key." This allows you to see when your eyes are distracted and when your head or body is ahead of the moment. Constantly adjusting focus and information based on staying present frees your mind and body from speculation, projection, and memory. This wasted energy then overloads you, which, in turn, speeds things up and makes decision making harder; your response time would slow, and mistakes and sloppy movements would appear. This is one aspect Ginn works during practice and training: "In rowing, we are less visual, but the sensory stuff for us internally is critical and the sensation of timing with partners is key to success. Being able to remain open but not overloaded requires some discrimination. It also seems to require a keen sense for softening, which relates to the gaze. Hard eyes are fixed on a point and are intense. I have played with soft eyes, and this allows a greater absorption of the environment . . . scanning body movement, fatigue, emotions, feelings, and thoughts. This is not for the purpose of dwelling on any single aspect, but to develop awareness. We must lighten our eyes, not trying to focus intensely permanently."

What is interesting here in rowing is that we find the same type of gaze as in tennis, the dead gaze: "Soft eyes is something we have worked on greatly. In a rowing boat it is like picking a point on the person in front or a spot on the back of the boat and then allowing all the information to come in. Awareness is open while we maintain clear intention, a focus."

**Rhythm and timing are some of the keys.
What is the best rhythm for you?**

**Do as gold medalists do:
Soften and lighten your eyes.**

---

*I sit quietly.
I breathe deeply.
I am focusing on nothing.
I am aware of everything.*

Body awareness

Passion is creativity of existence. It allows us to do everything with love. The body plays an essential part. Because without the body nothing happens. First of all we have to be aware of what the body tells us. It always send out important signals. And if one takes the time and pay attention to them, one progresses much faster and much further in this adventure. The body takes part entirely in the events, as much as the spirit, the mind and the emotions. So the thing is to try and reach this fluidity, flexibility and harmony in the gesture.

—Hélène Grimaud

Directing our gaze at the right place can create kinesthetic awareness, an ideal condition for being fully in our movements; it's therefore essential to entering the Zone. From his experience as a coach and trainer of distance runners and triathletes, Dean Hebert notes the importance of trusting the kinesthetic sense. Connecting to the kinesthetic channel allows better balance, coordination, and rhythm. If we focus on one aspect of sensitivity, such as balance, other aspects are also being developed. And to focus on our sensations is also to be adaptable, as Carrie Cheadle, coach and sports psychologist, says: "Zone might be defined as getting the mind and the body to work together to perform to that athlete's potential. In this case, you have to have some proficiency at the sport you are performing in. Proficiency in sport includes both the mind and the body. Kinesthetic awareness is an important skill to have because it allows the athlete to be able to make the necessary adjustments to their form, a key factor to stay in the Zone."

But Julie Bouteraon, a coach specializing in mental preparation, stresses the need to distinguish between the "mental and the physical sensations [required] to enter the Zone, and those of the Zone itself." That is a simple but key observation, because a lot of mental training manuals confuse the two.

Some have examined the role of our sensations, and more specifically the link between technique and sensations. This is the case of Sir John Whitmore, former race-car driver and adept of Tim Gallwey's Inner Game. This link is indeed a great challenge for coaches. The challenge lies in the answer to the question: "Are we seeking a correct technique or an optimal biomechanical efficiency?" Correct technique is traditionally instilled from the outside by an expert, but a real biomechanical effectiveness depends on the quality of kinesthetic feedback. Seeking out the Zone will therefore increase the player's kinesthetic feedback to generate an optimal technique—we could say from inside to outside.

Beyond our vision and our physical sensations, awareness of the entire body occurs in the Zone. Many people focus on the mind as a way to access the Zone, but often forget their body. Our senses, in their own way, contribute to producing an optimum state, but it is our whole body that will carry us into the Zone, especially through our movements. Indeed, our sixth sense, often forgotten, is the sense of the movement, which is at the forefront in the Zone. It seems that the greatest champions instinctively know how their body reacts by tapping into their sensations.

Of course, sport is not the only access to the Zone through the body. Other activities like music, by the mastery of gesture, or dance that is based on rhythmic and harmonious movements, can naturally lead to this state. More broadly, we seek to achieve this harmony between body and spirit in all activities of our lives.

Reconnect your mind and your body.

Your movements can guide you to the Zone.

**The rhythm of your body drives
the rhythm of your thoughts.**

---

*I stand quietly and breathe slowly,
feeling my breath move through my heart.*

Posture and rhythm

What I dream of is an art of balance . . .
—Henri Matisse

The relationship to the body is one of the bases of all martial arts, especially postural control. By simply moving your body in a deliberately loose and fluid way, as in Tai Chi, you can induce a state of mental calm and physical control while remaining alert. Our emotional state and our body language—therefore our posture—are closely linked. Thus, our movements and our posture affect our mental state, which in turn has a direct impact on our performance.

A better posture also brings us the better balance needed to reach the Zone. If you experience competition in any sport, you quickly learn that balance is the key. Our posture, particularly led by the movements and positions of the head, plays a major role in our movement and in our mind. The head initiates the movements that affect the quality of our vision, which in turn is intimately connected to our attention. A right placement of the head can therefore both initiate movement and provide quality vision.

Once we've reached a balance through better posture, we find a good rhythm and good timing. This rhythm goes beyond the body. Jim Loehr says that during games, Ivan Lendl "adopted a long series of rituals between the points which helped him to maintain his concentration and rhythm."

Being in the Zone is also to set the rhythm or to keep the rhythm with the elements, the wave, or the game. For François Castell, mental trainer and ultra-runner, it is essential: "It is the rhythm of the body, of course, but also the rhythm of thoughts. It seems that the flow of thoughts takes that of our body." American golfer Lee Trevino summarizes this perfectly: "The Zone is the tempo."

Balance.

Take the time to read *Zone Mind, Zone Body* by Roy Palmer.

I get into the rhythm.
Balance is power.

Breathing

"You cannot do it," explained the Master, *"because you do not breathe right."*

—Eugene Herrigel

The activity most beneficial to performance—breathing.

—Roy Palmer

Quiet your breathing, focus your attention on the center of your consciousness. You will master senses, emotion and mind.

—Bhagavad Gita

The body in balance is always in rhythm, and this rhythm is first that of our breath. Breathing can serve as a link between body and mind because focusing on it, its rhythm, its physical sensations, necessarily anchors us in the present. The breath is linked to our mind, as Dr. Jacob Liberman has noted: "Everything changes, especially the external parameters we need to anchor ourselves in the present of something always accessible. Our breathing is here to help us. It also gives us direct feedback from our body."

Breath control has always been a central point of the oldest spiritual traditions. Yogis and Zen and martial arts masters have all attached great importance to breathing properly. This knowledge has been naturally transmitted to sports. Western athletes often integrate relaxation and breathing exercises into their preparation. It's little surprise that breathing is always at the center of the various approaches to reaching the Zone. You will say, yes, it's déjà vu. But honestly, who really takes the time to do it? Who takes time to focus on the most essential task for the body—breathing?

Zone experiences are common among athletes, but they become even more common at a high level where the ability to enter in a state of kinesthetic awareness is essential. Many athletes show an intense concentration on their sensations. This is the case of John Sieben, gold medal winner in the two-hundred-meter butterfly at the Los Angeles Olympics: "The first half of the race I have really few memories of. Because I got a good start and I just went into what I had mentally rehearsed. I was just swimming within my body and focused on how my body felt." Jade Edmiston, who beat the record for the fifty-meter breaststroke in 2004, shares one of her moments in the Zone: "At the time I felt less nervous than normal about winning this event, and more detached from the outcome. I was not really thinking too much. I sort of knew inside what was going to happen because I felt so in control. There was an inner sense of knowing. The only way of explaining it is that it was like the inside of my body, and my heart and everything felt like I was smiling on the inside. My whole body just felt like it was smiling." These testimonials make Jean-Philippe Vaillant, a specialist in mental training for tennis and golf, saying that it is important to "think with the body": "We need to learn how to think better in kinesthetic and visual ways."[24] But this approach hasn't fully emerged yet. As George Leonard remarked thirty-five years ago in his book *The Ultimate Athlete:* "Even the subject of psychological motivation was approached mechanically, as you program a computer. The body as instrument. Research and training for coaches and physical-education instructors focuses tightly on performance at the expense of experience. Instructors ask how many times a boy or girl can chin, but not how it feels to chin, how it is."[25] Yet this body awareness has long been taught in the martial arts, where you learn to focus your energy on the body's center of gravity, located a few inches below the navel and thought to be the source of any energy and movement.

Take time to breathe. Slow down and let go.

Your breath is the link between your body and your mind.

Observe how much better your vision is when you breathe properly.

Just breathe.

To let go

To dispose of the body's daily habits is to give yourself a chance at another relation to the mind.
—Hélène Grimaud

To know our body is one of the first steps toward experiencing the Zone. Once aware of his body and confident in his abilities, the athlete may be more detached. This detachment is often expressed by the idea of letting go. When he broke the barrier of the four-minute mile, Roger Bannister was feeling "completely detached." Some things cannot be enforced. You must release or free yourself and let them occur. We don't try to fall asleep; we just let go. Similarly, to be successful, you don't have to consciously try to focus on winning; you just have to be absorbed in the experience. To let go is to finally trust your body, surrendering to the movement, being absorbed by the task, separating from the result and being only in the present. Chris Evert summarizes it well: "It's that knowledge, that confidence, and also that freedom

of just letting go, letting the strokes flow." And the undis-
puted master of letting go is Tim Gallwey, author of *The
Inner Game of Tennis*,[26] which says in essence: Knowing when
to think and when to let go is the key for tennis at the peak
of your potential.

Thomas Sorensen, a researcher at the University of
Copenhagen, thinks that it's important in the Zone to stop
the continuous monitoring of the quality of our performance—that is, our constant evaluations: "I think a highly
trained athlete enters the Zone when motoring does not
detect errors for an extended period." This vision is shared
by Andy Clark, a researcher at the University of Edinburgh:
"I think that one currently undervalued key to understanding
flow is understanding that the brain and body share a single
goal, which is to minimize informational surprise. The brain
does it by encoding good models of the situation. The body
can move so as to give the brain the inputs it is best able to
predict and handle. When we are in the zone, we are doing
this so well that no error signal (corresponding to surprise) is
being created." When we are in the Zone, no error signal is
detected. We must therefore abandon control, to have more

. . . control! Paradox? Not really. It's actually a matter of abandoning conscious and intentional control, and letting the intuitive mind take over. This mind has control over most small muscle movements, and it works the fastest.

Let go.

I just let go of what I am not.

Tim Gallwey and the Inner Game

These shots, it's like someone else was playing for me. In these moments, I say: "It's time, you need it, take the risk, try something." It is a kind of dialogue between me, the player and another player, who would be the coach, the consultant.

—Roger Federer

While some know Tim Gallwey's bestseller *The Inner Game of Tennis*,[27] his approach is often quickly summarized as: "We must watch the ball!" However, his message is actually quite different.

Gallwey was captain of the tennis team at Harvard, then worked in an experimental college until 1969. In August 1971 he went to India and spent some time in an ashram, where he learned to calm his mind through meditation. When Gallwey returned to the United States, he began to implement his vision for sport and the techniques of meditation. At first he called his method "Yoga Tennis"; he renamed his approach "the Inner Game" as he wrote. The book's success showed that some common doubts and frustrations on the sports field were not being addressed by conventional methods.

Tim Gallwey advocates what he calls "relaxed concentration"—the spontaneous performance that occurs only when the mind is relaxed and seems to be one with the body. When this happens on a tennis court, we are focused without trying. We do what must be done without having to apply ourselves excessively. We feel that we move perfectly, all without effort. The aim of the "Inner Game" is to increase the frequency and duration of those moments when the shots seem to come naturally, when our subconscious takes over. In those moments we feel we have been "lucky," but they are in fact brief moments of Zone. Our immersion in the action requires all our energy and leaves the unconscious and automatic functions to take place without the intervention of thoughts. We have the sensation that the mind is partly disconnected. But to play "unconsciously" does not mean without being conscious of everything: quite the opposite! Being in the Zone is in fact to have a greater awareness of our surroundings—in tennis, the opponent and the ball—while not being concerned about technical issues or thoughts about the past or what could happen.

The hardest part is calming and silencing the conscious mind. Calming the mind means less thinking, calculating, judging, worrying, fear; fewer expectations; less effort, less regret, less control. Because to try to control the Zone is immediately to lose it. To help us understand this idea, Gallwey discusses the two "Selves" that appear whenever we are on the tennis court. Self 1, the conscious mind, judges and gives instructions on how to play, while Self 2, the one who does, automatically and unconsciously, receives these instructions and executes them. Tim Gallwey's idea is that to play at your peak, you need to silence Self 1 and so release Self 2. In order to bypass the type of conscious thoughts that are on the path of the Zone and to anchor yourself in the present, he advises naturally focusing your attention on breathing; then during the game vision takes over.

We can summarize his method in four main steps. First: Observe your current behavior and feelings without judgment. Second: Ask your body to program positive images and sensations. It's a return to your senses: See, feel, and realize what really is. Step three: Let go. And finally, the fourth step: No judgment about your performance. To develop this ability to let the unconscious express itself is to rediscover the natural way to learn that we all experienced when we learned to walk or to talk as a child.

Don't try. Just do.

Find your Inner Game:
Observe without judging.
Choose positive images and sensations.
Let go and do.
Don't judge your performance.

Take the time to read *The Inner Game of Tennis* by Tim Gallwey.

I watch the clouds come and go.

Conscious, unconscious

You can't hit and think at the same time.
—Yogi Berra

I have discovered, again and again,
that I usually know what I need to do but just deny it . . .
—Mark Nepo

To let go is to make room for the unconscious. A feature of the Zone that recurs in descriptions is the feeling of being on autopilot: In the Zone everything works without any conscious effort to control it. Athletes say it is instinctive or natural. A good image of the sensations we can experience when we are beyond our technique is driving: We're not thinking about what we're do and often not thinking of anything specific, yet we're aware, seeing everything and nothing at the same time.

The Zone is therefore a mental state in which the thinking part of the brain, the cerebral cortex, is short-circuited. The brain operates automatically at a primitive level, while being fully engaged. Mark McGrath, an Australian movement specialist, says it well: "We have in us, deeply entrenched, older programs and more stable operating so that the body can move automatically."

Why make room for the unconscious? Simply because our unconscious mind sees the big picture and collects information from the senses without judgment. In fact, the unconscious mind drives the body; you speak to it very often! Most important, it comes when you are trying to automate your movements. Thus, once we've learned movement sequences through repetition, we do not need to perform them consciously. However, this does not mean that we must completely leave our conscious mind. This mind is essential for analyzing the situation and selecting appropriate strategies, but it is too slow for action. When it's time to move, shoot, or hit, the intuitive mind must take over. So in the Zone, there is no room for thought. Japanese baseball players have also their own word for this: *mushin,* which refers to a mind that is not attached to a thought or an emotion yet is open to everything. This concept is well illustrated by the famous quote from baseball player Yogi Berra: "You can't think and hit the ball at the same time."

In his book on tennis and the mind, Jean-Philippe Vaillant explains the importance of our subconscious: "There is no distinction between what the player does and what he thinks. It does not mean that the player is not aware of what he is doing. He doesn't think consciously and rationally. He is in a state of high sensory awareness."[28] The assumption here is that in the Zone, the body is not hindered by conscious thoughts; it instinctively makes the right choice. This mode of operation is the basis of the Inner Game of Tim Gallwey.

To reach this state, a key suggestion is to spend some of our training sessions on developing our unconscious side— learning to play without thinking. We can act quickly—more quickly than our conscious mind works. This applies, for example, to tennis during the return of serve or when both players are at the net. The aim is to focus only on what happens, on the action. We must let our unconscious do what we have learned during hours of training. Take care of the process and the result will take care of itself! In short, we could say: Let's trust what we already know! *Avatar* fans may remember "I have to trust my body to know what to do," which summarizes that essential idea.

Trusting the unconscious was described a long time ago by Eugen Herrigel. He learned archery from a Zen master, who taught him: "You should not shoot the arrow. The arrow should leave the bow by itself. The move will be smooth only when it takes the archer by surprise." This is why the Zone is outside our control. Just as we can't fall asleep more quickly by closing our eyes harder—we also can't enter the Zone directly by trying.

You already know what to do.

I expect nothing.
I am prepared for anything.

A Zen Zone?

The world is ruled by letting things take their course.

—Lao-tsu

Be happy for this moment. This moment is your life.

—Omar Khayyám

Attention control, body awareness, and breathing are essential features of the Zone. They are also the foundations of all Eastern disciplines. The French writer Denis Grozdanovitch[29] recalls the words of Bernard Grasset, who, in "Letter to an Athlete on Style," dwells on this idea: "[With] a good look at most inspired great players, I almost always found (at least in the decisive moments of the game) the kind of powers of concentration where it seems that the will plays no role. I often asked myself if this mental state—which the athletes apparently rediscovered by intuition—is not the same one advocated in Eastern thought by the masters of martial arts."[30] The central aspect of martial arts has indeed always been training and mastery of the mind. We also find in *The Art of War* by Sun Tzu, or Taoist books such as I Ching and the Tao Te Ching, the principles for developing what is sometimes called "mental strength." These books taught us twenty-five hundred years ago the importance of being in the present and following our feelings and intuitions. The popular new approach known as neuro-linguistic programming (NLP) has invented nothing!

Geoff Mangum, golf coach, is a good example of someone who first became interested in neuroscience and then made the link with the Eastern wisdom: "The quickest way toward harmony between body and mind is to ignore the mind and just perform with our body. It is a kind of Zen." After more than thirty years spent with athletes, as well as astronauts, musicians, and surgeons, sports psychologist Dr. Terry Orlick also makes a clear link between the Eastern wisdom of Zen and the Zone. For him, the two terms describe the same experience: "One of the greatest lessons that I have learned from great performers is the oneness or absolute connection that they have with what they are doing, seeing, feeling, or creating. Entering the Zen zone means becoming one with and inseparable from the essence of what you are doing during the moment that you are doing it."[31]

As noted by Joe Parent, a coach on the professional golf tour, the parallel between the characteristics of Zen and the Zone is surprising: "Zen means 'action with awareness,' being completely in the present moment. The qualities that accompany the Zen experience include expansive vision, effortless focus, a feeling of equanimity and timelessness, abundant confidence, and complete freedom from anxiety or doubt. Interestingly, this is exactly the way champion athletes describe 'being in the Zone.'"[32] It is almost funny to see the efforts researchers make just to give new words to these old experiences and methods!

However, this similarity is not yet widely recognized. Mike Murphy, a pioneer of Zone research, has said: "Western training programs are not grounded in a philosophy that encourages the systematic development of unusual forces. The Eastern martial arts, however, have methods for mobilizing energy by uniting mind and body. Their techniques are embedded in a view that unusual energy is accessible to us all. In Japan such energy is called ki, in China ch'i, in India prana. Like yoga, the martial arts teach methods for deliberately tapping it. Some writers use the word *intrinsic* to differentiate this inner resource from energy that is produced by muscles."

Be one with what you do.

Take the time to read the *Tao Te Ching,* and *In Pursuit of Excellence* by Terry Orlick.

Now is the moment.

Phil Jackson:
a Zen master in the NBA

Do not hold back. Play the way you live your life with your whole heart and soul.
—Phil Jackson

Basketball is a sport that involves the subtle interweaving of players at full speed to the point where they are thinking and moving as one.
—Phil Jackson, *Sacred Hoops*

Phil Jackson, the famous coach of the Chicago Bulls and Los Angeles Lakers, is probably one of the best coaches ever. Jackson's critics are sometimes quick to claim that he has been fortunate enough to coach Michael Jordan, Shaquille O'Neal, and Kobe Bryant. But one thing is certain: He gets the maximum potential from his players, and for that he doesn't use academic methods! In fact, he's created a new approach toward sports that combines the best of Western and Eastern wisdom. He has detailed in several books[33] the influences that have shaped his unique approach.

In college he became interested in Eastern philosophies, especially Buddhism and Native American wisdom; he even worked on Indian reservations during summers. Describing his approach, Phil Jackson says: "It encompasses the attitude that Zen is a way to integrate mind and body, sport and spiritual." *Spiritual* is a word rarely used in sport by coaches and journalists. Jackson doesn't care, and he has certainly succeeded given his ten NBA championships!

He meditates every day to find peace and harmony for him and his team. He has introduced this meditation to his players, who practice in groups and understand quickly that it is the heart of Jackson's system. All the staff focus on the fact that to achieve your best performance, you must be relaxed. And to cultivate this relaxed state, they practice meditation.

Players sit, quiet and still, with their eyes open and focus on their breathing. The purpose of this exercise is to achieve calm and quiet mind, with full attention and consciousness in the moment. Just before Game Seven of the NBA playoffs in June 2010, Lakers coaches focused on relaxing the players instead of increasing their adrenaline. The team gathered in a room, Phil Jackson said few words, the lights dimmed, the players were nearly asleep. "Just a quiet meditation," explains coach assistant Jim Cleamons, "in order for them to understand the business at hand for that evening. If we're going through some turbulent times, to help us get focused."

"Before the lights are turned off," says the other assistant coach, Chuck Person, "there are a thousand things going through your mind. A thousand thoughts, personal, basketball-wise, or anything else. You start to focus on that breath, everything goes away. You're in complete darkness. It's just you and that breath. And when the lights come on you feel relaxed, you feel rejuvenated, and you have a rejuvenation period that carries forward onto the court." While the Lakers' staff is convinced that meditation gives them an advantage over their opponents, the concept remains strange for most people. A journalist asked Glen Davis, coach of the Celtics, about what the opponents were going to do before the decisive Game Seven: "The Lakers staff is convincing that meditation offers a major advantage, and one any team might consider employing. So . . . do the Celtics do the same thing? I told Glen Davis what his opponents will be doing before Game 7: 'They meditate?' he replied, his face scrunched up in confusion. 'In the dark? What is that? They just sit there? For real? . . . Naw, I ain't trying that. If that's what they do to get ready for the game, hey: Whatever floats your boat.'"[34]

And what Jackson has learned, he shares with his team. He is thus well known for offering his players books very important to him, such as *Zen Mind, Beginner's Mind* by Shunryu Suzuki. One day, Jackson gave Shaquille O'Neal a book by Aristotle, which emphasizes that excellence is achieved by habit and repetition. Jackson wanted to send the message that by practicing more regularly, O'Neal would be able to perform better under pressure. This idea of repetition is of course not new—but integrating it with life is, and O'Neal was able to do it. Soon after, Big Shaq started calling himself the Big Aristotle! Phil Jackson has said: "He knew that . . . I was sending him a message. The book basically says, you know, this is something that corresponds to where you're at in your life, and can I connect with you at this intellectual level. And what I tell them is it's nice to have a companion besides the TV when you're on the road . . . [You can] read it before you go to bed at night and understand that there is another world that can open up to you in your intellectual imagination."

He reveals how he led his players to act with a clear mind, without thinking, just doing it, staying in the moment, staying calm and focused in the middle of chaos: "Athletes who are not tense at times of stress are in the flow. Basketball is a matter of skill. Being able to move quickly. Shooting is a matter of viewing and focusing. All this comes with the presence of a clear mind and spirit. Comfort can play an important role in success."

At first the players are surprised, like Horace Grant: "Phil has a tendency to do weird things." And the first time Jackson asked the Chicago Bulls to meditate, he noted that Michael Jordan looked at his teammates to see if they agreed—and was surprised to see that they did! Of course, not everyone feels this way. This is the case with Kobe Bryant: "I don't know why Phil keeps giving me those books; he knows I'm not going to read them." And with Ron Harper: "I didn't read none of them. I got six books now. Let me see. Yeah, six books. So, in my older age, I got something to read!" Even Jordan spoke of his "Zen-Buddhist stuff." But ultimately, Jackson's approach commands respect. Kobe Bryant: "Sometimes you might not know exactly what he's talking about but you still listen."

Jackson works to develop in his players an awareness of everything around them, as well as of themselves. Thus, in *Time* magazine, Kobe Bryant said: "It sounds like a minor thing, but it's very big when you're playing at this level to really be aware of everything around you." One of Jackson's players told a reporter, "He has this way of getting you to give yourself to something you never thought of before. We do Tai Chi and yoga and meditate. I never did these things before, never thought of them. And maybe there's no direct correlation between these things and basketball. But it broadens our horizons. It challenges us."[35]

Beyond relaxation, Jackson tries to develop in his players "an intuitive feel for how their movements and those of everyone on the floor are interconnected." He creates this connection through breathing. Sometimes during games, instead of talking to his players, giving technical advice, he asks them to remember their sessions and join together to "share a breath." So when things get stressful, the whole team takes time to just breathe. This state of mind begins on the morning in the meeting room. Says Chuck Person: "He teaches you how to find your way in the maze, in the chaos. You can always go back and find yourself with that breath. I've learned during anxious moments, since I have been here with the Lakers, that that breath is very important to take to center yourself. Players do it. They get together, take a breath, collect their thoughts, so they can perform . . . We're going to take our breath and we're going to have one mind, one collective breath, and we're going to go out there and do it together. Phil teaches that, and he's great to learn from."

Jackson teaches how to be in the moment: "Basketball happens at such a fast pace that your mind has a tendency to race at the same speed as your pounding heart. As the pressure builds, it's easy to start thinking too much. But if you're always trying to figure the game out, you won't be able to respond creatively to what's going on. Yogi Berra once said about baseball: 'How can you think and hit at the same time?' The same is true with basketball, except everything's happening much faster. The key is seeing and doing. If you're focusing on anything other than reading the court and doing what needs to be done, the moment will pass you by." But beyond this, the approach also teaches players to love the moment. And when they succeed, "Everybody is activated, and good things start happening. It's interesting—the other players are consciously aware of the fact that they're anticipating their teammates' behavior. Somehow, mysteriously, they just know the timing is right. They simply feel something out ahead of themselves and make their move. It's not an out-of-body experience or anything like that. They just feel the tremendous pull of an activity, of what has to happen next."[36]

He continues, "What we try to do with our group is breathe together, share the same space, find something outside just playing basketball on the court. This 'spiritual stuff' brings an act of community to us."[37]

Jackson's entire philosophy can perhaps be summarized in his famous line: "Don't hold back. Play the way you live your life, with your whole heart and soul."

Turbulent times are the best times to meditate.

**Find the type of meditation that fits your
mind and body. Do you need to be active?
Do you prefer to sit quietly?**

**Feel that your movements are connected
to the world.**

Take a breath.

**Love the moment and
let the good things happen!**

Take the time to read
Zen Mind, Beginner's Mind by Shunryu Suzuki.

I breathe deeply and smile.

Yoga and Zone

It makes sense to think of Yoga as a very thoroughly planned flow activity.

—Mihaly Csikszentmihalyi

The states that athletes reach in the Zone are similar to those meditation states we see in yoga. Mihaly Csikszentmihalyi, a professor at Claremont University in California who specializes in positive psychology and is famous for having introduced the concept of "flow," notes the parallels among flow, yoga, and martial arts: "In many respects, what the West has accomplished in terms of harnessing material energy is matched by what India and the Far East have achieved in terms of direct control of consciousness."[38]

Among the greatest Eastern methods to train the body, one of the oldest and the most widespread is the practice known as Hatha yoga. It is interesting to take a closer look at some of the steps in this discipline, since they correspond to the psychology of the "flow" (the process) and the Zone.

The goal of yoga is to unify body and consciousness. To achieve this goal, the basic texts of yoga, compiled fifteen hundred years ago, suggest eight stages. The first two are a preparation for changing your attitudes. They involve increasing awareness before you begin attempting mind control. In practice, this involves retaining your actions and thoughts. The second stage is following specific routines to channel your attention and thus make it easier to control. The next two levels involve physical preparation and the development of habits that will help you overcome the demands of your body and focus without being tired or distracted.

The third level consists of practicing of various postures (asanas) without succumbing to fatigue. This is the stage of yoga that we all know in Western society. The fourth level is breath control (pranayama), which aims to relax the body and to stabilize the rhythm of breathing. The fifth level is the hinge between the preparatory exercises and the practice of yoga itself. It involves learning to withdraw our attention from external objects by directing our senses—and thus we become able to see, hear, and feel only what we wish to have enter our consciousness. Already at this level we are close to the goal of yoga and flow: to achieve control over what happens in the mind.

The next three levels aim to control consciousness by purely mental operations anchored on previous physical techniques. First is the ability to concentrate for long periods on a single stimulus.

Think of the first stages this way: First we learn to keep things out of our minds; then we learn to keep them in. Intense meditation is the next level. Here we learn to forget the self in uninterrupted concentration. Finally, the last stage is when the meditator and the object of meditation become one.

We can see that these different levels correspond with modern techniques available for achieving flow and thus the Zone. All aim to control consciousness at a higher and higher level. Csikszentmihalyi explains: "The similarities between Yoga and flow are extremely strong; in fact it makes sense to think of Yoga as a very thoroughly planned flow activity. Both try to achieve a joyous, self-forgetful involvement through concentration, which in turn is made possible by discipline of the body."

He logically concludes: "It is not unreasonable to regard Yoga as one of the oldest and most systematic methods of producing the flow experience."

Learn the Sun Salute.
Do it every day.
When you do, focus on your
breath and your rhythm.

My mind is calm.
I have the energy and passion
to make my thoughts reality.

Don't do

The perfect talk is without word.
The perfect action is to not act.
—Lao-tzu

Do nothing and then nothing is left to be undone.
—Lao-tzu

A basic concept of Zen—as well as one of the signatures of the Zone—is to go beyond the technique and to allow our subconscious to take control. This is the famous "do without doing."[39] To abandon all control, to not do, may seem strange when we are accustomed to a wealth of admonitions to *do it*. But to not do is not to give up and to do nothing. Rather, it is to do nothing *forced*, and to avoid thoughts that could lead you away from your experience. It is therefore less a question of learning something new than one of unlearning something old and irrelevant—in other words, getting rid of our habit of analyzing everything and wanting to control everything. The way to access these states of consciousness is therefore to abandon our old patterns and to trust our body and our instinct.

What are your old patterns of thinking?
Please, stop analyzing everything!

I let go and everything falls into place.

Quiet mind

Don't think. Then you'll begin to know the Way.
—Zhuangzi

No amount of thinking can stop thinking.
—Mark Nepo

Mike Lardon[40] came to the conclusion that the Zone in its simplest form is a condition in which the mind is empty and quiet, a bit like when you are sitting at the movie theater or driving a car while thinking about everything and nothing at the same time. However, there are situations where your mind can be in the present, thinking of movement, and yet not be in sync with your body. This applies to golf, for instance. Joe Parent warns: "If you think about your swing, your mind is in your head, with ideas such as how you should swing, rather than in your body."[41] This is one of the reasons why the Zone disappears when we realize we're in it: "Thinking about something implies a quality of separation, in the same way that looking at something requires some separation between observer and object. We may even feel like our thinking mind is in our head, watching our body. That's why when we're thinking about our swing, body and mind are not synchronized. Body is swinging, but mind is thinking about swinging and therefore separate from it." He adds: "During your swing is not the time to give yourself a lesson. Players often rely on swing thoughts, but thinking while swinging isn't such a good idea. It's preferable to have a swing image, one that includes at least the path and finishing point of the ball, but can also include the feel of the swing."

When was the last time your mind and body were in sync?

Keep it simple

Simplicity is the final thing. After having conquered all difficulties, after having played a huge quantity of notes, it is simplicity that emerges with all its charm as the final seal of art. It is not an easy thing.
—Frédéric Chopin

Enjoy the little things in life, for one day you may look back and realize they were the big things.
—Antonio Smith

The key may lie in simplicity. This is in fact the keyword of David Breslow, a mental trainer for several players on the golf pro tour. He doesn't use the usual framework of sports psychology in his work; he considers it too complicated for athletes, who don't need to be overloaded with theories that often create overanalysis: "When science separates mind, body, and vision, she cuts the analysis things too: precisely what we do not need to reach the Zone! The Zone is not always achieved by having more information!" Thus, like some coaches, he teaches us mainly to be aware of our body, mind, and emotions, a process that does not actually require more information.

Dan Millman, a former trampoline champion, is a long-time university coach and author of the bestsellers *The Inner Athlete*[42] and *The Peaceful Warrior*.[43] He also insists on the importance of simplicity in the techniques we use and also in our expectations: no complex theories or complicated techniques and languages. Dan is attached to the fundamentals, which for him are breathing and meditation: "Such epiphanic moments, or sometimes series of moments, are the result of the conjunction of numerous elements, some known, predictable, and developmental, and others random, subtle and chance coincidence. My own work focuses on what is more controllable—variables like concentration, visualization and practice, which perhaps enhance or encourage greater odds of achieving that state . . . Every athlete knows that in some moments she or he is more 'on' and other times, not. I don't personally believe that athletes can significantly increase those moments—but in the simplest and most ordinary terms, performance (and mental focus, concentration, absorption, immersion) may be a natural result of conscious training of one-pointed attention. Studying meditators (including athletes and martial artists who develop a meditative type focus in their movement) may be fruitful. The martial arts have indeed long been able to find connections between body and mind, simple ways to reconnect." He adds: "We can make the link between the Zone and the state experienced in the martial arts, especially the moments of 'satori' when the mind, emotions and body are in a particular state of harmony, of integrity and synergy."

Millman emphasizes the quality of diet, exercise, and rest—three key points that guide our bodies into an optimal state—sleeping, eating, moving, action! Is this too simple? Maybe not, because it is surely in building on those pillars that we can access the Zone more often. With his simplicity of language, and in the face of sports science and new technology giving us access to brain function in real time, Dan Millman's approach can perhaps be seen as simplistic. Yet I believe that instead, it offers analogies to our relationship to the body and the mind–body connection.

Through his books and movie, Millman has touched people around the world by showing that the Zone is not something that is achieved. Instead, this state is within us; it belongs to us. Through the paths that life offers to us—and sport is one of those paths—we can reconnect to the Zone inside.

Be honest with yourself:
Do you sleep enough?
What about the quality of your diet?

Think about what helps you feel "on" or "off."

Take the time to read *Way of the Peaceful Warrior* by Dan Millman.

Simplify your life.

From instinct to intuition

Intuition is really a sudden immersion of the soul into the universal current of life.
—Paulo Coelho, *The Alchemist*

The only real valuable thing is intuition.
—Albert Einstein

A warrior of light knows that he will hear an order in the silence of his heart that will guide him.
—Paulo Coelho, *Manual of the Warrior of Light*

Keeping it simple means questioning yourself less about how to do and more about how to make room for intuition. *Intuition* is not a word that scientists like very much; for them it is simply the result of automation. The athlete develops a kind of mental model for typical situations encountered in his sport. Yet some athletes in the Zone report something closer to premonition. This is the case of Bill Russell, former

Boston Celtics player: "During these moments I could feel the next move even before the other team put the ball in. I played many times in feeling very well, but once there I really had chills."[44]

We know that champions use the best external information to help them anticipate, but Drew Ginn, triple Olympic rowing champion, says that in the Zone this goes far beyond. He relates an experience at the world championships in 2000:

It is possible to be aware of the movements of opponents, of their intention. My intuition was telling me that every thing was going to be ok and that this first race would be easy. My mind was trying to tell me something else, but I remember feeling it was just chatter. Then I looked out of our boat and saw the British pair sitting next to us and in one moment I knew that they would not be faster than us. It is hard to explain what it was; I had an insight and felt that we would perform optimally. Now, the thing is that the British pair were the world champs from the previous year, and both had been successful in the Sydney Olympics in the coxless four. The history and results they had between them were and still are remarkable, but on that day and in fact the whole weekend of competition I had a wonderful sense of knowing we would be the fastest pair.

On the occasions when I have accessed deep intuition, it has involved sensing the next step without
needing to know what the next step is. This may
seem paradoxical, but I have found that it is when I
have let go of needing that things become clear. The
clarity is a beautiful thing and free from confusion.

This ability to sense an event before it happens often
occurs during episodes of great emotional stress and high
physical risk. Extreme sports are often the scene of such
episodes. Tony Ray, extreme surfer, says[45]: "Being able to tune
into your 6th sense and intuition is a really big part of it I
think. There are definitely times when I trust my intuition. If
I don't feel right I won't go out in the water. If it is really big
and dangerous and my intuition is saying don't go out I just
go and hide somewhere. I pretend I didn't know. I am lucky
I don't have that kind of pressure on me to have to go out all
the time, which is good. When dealing with those really
intense wipe out situations you sort of just do it intuitively—
you have that intuitive knowledge of what to do in the
situation, where to go and where to put your body."

And this intuition seems to grow if we make it one of the
goals of our training. As Drew Ginn says: "We can develop

our intuition. Many times in the past I have found after the fact that . . . intuitively I was on track and from these experiences I have worked on developing trust in it. Practicing being aware of these moments has been my focus. Deep intuition tells me that when I accept the natural flow, the motion and emotion and allow it to pass through me, I am able to face any challenge."[46]

When was the last time you trusted your intuition—in sport or in life?

Be aware of the signs around you.

Do you know what synchronicities are? Learn to be aware of them; they will always guide you.

Take the time to read *The Alchemist* by Paulo Coelho.

I let my intuitions lead me.

Effortless

Follow the path of least resistance if you want to be victorious.
—Sun Tzu

The feeling of ease and letting go that athletes describe requires a different approach to movement. In fact, watching someone in the Zone is seeing someone who has evolved beyond technical mastery, and this translates into physical terms through economy or even absence of effort. We have already seen that it corresponds to reduced activity in the brain. However, the modern approach to training is based on the stress–recovery cycle, which leads us to push (via repetition) to our limits and then let the body recover. This is how we are supposed to become stronger and faster. Thus, conventional training requires an enormous amount of effort. On the other side, the Zone is an effortless experience. If we want to reproduce it, perhaps it would be better to seek to emulate its qualities? Perhaps it would be better to cultivate this effortless state, rather than pushing the body to its limits?

This is precisely one of the strategies advocated by Dr. John Douillard: "Enter the Zone ease from the first moment of each drive, and then build on that experience without separating the mind from the body."[47] This is also the workhorse of Roy Palmer, who teaches cricket, practices martial arts, and fights the idea that we can reach the Zone through effort. He simply observes that most often people report an effortless sensation when they are in the Zone. He thinks that we try too hard with current training methods, and therefore we interfere with what should be a natural process. He explains how training techniques can unwittingly push us away from the Zone: "I believe that continued use of such techniques creates the habit of applying excessive muscular effort and control in areas where they are not required. Consequently this will interfere with the naturally coordinated and efficient movement associated with being in the Zone. If the sensations experienced in the Zone are what it feels like for every part of our body to be working at its optimum, then all our training should work toward this."[48]

With this idea Palmer joins Eugene Herrigel, who was among the first in Western society to try to penetrate the heart of Zen theory and practice by studying archery with a Zen master for six years and sharing his experiences. He highlights the importance of going beyond technique in order to reach what he calls "art without effort."[49]

The key is indeed for athletes to work with a minimum of conscious effort by using their instincts. It's a vision shared by Dr. Jerry Lynch, sports psychologist: "The way to achieve victory is through more effective strategies to eliminate or minimize resistance. It is the art of 'effortless effort.'"[50] In Chinese, this paradox of effortless effort is called *wu-wei,* meaning "not doing what is not natural." As our training helps us develop muscle memory via repetition of movement, the body learns how to move without having to think about it.

Is your face relaxed when you run, play, move, hit, or jump?

Remember your last effortless experience.

Take the time to read Thinking Body, Dancing Mind by Jerry Lynch and Chungliang Al Huang.

I am relaxed.
I feel relaxed.
I smile.

To be a child again

Childlikeness has to be restored with long years of training in the art of self-forgetfulness. When this is attained, man does his great works. He thinks yet he does not think.
—Daisetz T. Suzuki

Be happy in the moment, that's enough. Each moment is all we need, not more.
—Mother Teresa

It takes a very long time to become young.
—Pablo Picasso

Do athletes learn to enter the Zone more often by increasing the connections corresponding to this experience in the brain? Or does this happen simply because they have never forgotten how they felt as children at play? If the latter is true, then the Zone is within us—a natural state lost after our childhood. The question is worth asking because when we observe children playing, we can really notice their relaxed bodies and ease of movement.

Mike Lardon is a psychiatrist specializing in sports at the University of California–San Diego, and works with many top athletes. He is one of those in the United States who has long sought to understand the Zone. He makes the link between the Zone and how we learned and played when we were kids: "When children play, they are completely engaged in the here and now. Their minds do not get stuck comparing themselves to their peers. They effortlessly transition their attention from one activity to the next, forgetting quickly what happened moments earlier and becoming completely absorbed in the present. They are able to make this transition seamlessly because their focus is on having fun and enjoying themselves."[51] We can also find the beginnings of an answer in ancient wisdom. The great Zen master Daisetz T. Suzuki said: "Man is a thinking reed but his great works are done when he is not calculating and thinking. 'Childlikeness' has to be restored with long years of training in the art of self-forgetfulness. When this is attained, man thinks yet he does not think."

Antoine de Saint-Exupéry has said: "All great people were first children, but few of them remember." In sport, it seems that champions remember much better! Here the main question is: How can we keep this incredible natural quality after becoming adults, when the majority of our activities (starting with school) are left-brain-oriented?

Be fully in the here and now.

Take the time to read *The Little Prince* by Antoine de Saint-Exupéry.

I am calm and in the moment.

The links

Dreams show you where you are and where you are going.
They reveal your destiny.
—Carl Jung

It's the possibility of having a dream come true that makes life
interesting.
—Paulo Coelho

You can't put a limit on anything. The more you dream, the
farther you get.
—Michael Phelps

We now know more about the Zone, but we've yet to discover the key allowing us to put everything together. Mastering body and vision are probably essential to entering the Zone, but how can we make straight this building that seems so fragile? Let's look at what might enable us to create that alchemy, because—in the words of a Zen master—

"Enlightenment is an accident, but some activities make you accident-prone."

First there is the idea that our dreams and visions are very important along the path to the Zone. That is surprisingly the first key point raised by scientist Mike Lardon. All great champions had from childhood a strong vision of their future success. They saw themselves winning and holding the trophy. This vision guides them and gives them incredible energy. This power of dreams is the power of images, as noted by Terry Orlick: "Your images lead your reality. They always have and always will."

To create, maintain, and feed a positive vision therefore helps us shape our dreams, transforming them into something real. This is reflected in the book *What Makes Winners Win* by journalist Charlie Jones through the testimony of Pat Riley, NBA coach, four-time champion with the Lakers: "That's what it's all about. It's about an image. It's about visualizing where you want to be and seeing yourself there someday. Every day you visualize it, you dream about it, you think about it, you work on it, and you keep striving for it."[52]

We can hold on to that dream by using pictures grouped

on a poster or in our computer, what some call a "vision board." It is a simple exercise but surprisingly powerful and effective.

The second link would be emotions. For Keith Henschen, professor of sports science at the University of Utah, entering the Zone always involves a combination of emotions and movements. Indeed, most of the great sports champions have a precious quality: They know when to pay attention to the physical and emotional messages that their bodies and minds communicate. In short, they are more attentive to their feelings and their emotions. And as we have seen, those who have already tasted the Zone are better able to live it again! Their first experience of the Zone left a strong imprint in their brains, which they can reactivate. Here, emotions play a dual role: to update this Zone and to anchor it deeply, making it easier to reproduce.

But the memory of their first Zone experience is also a risk for athletes, who may attempt without success to live this state again, trying to find the same conditions that created it previously. The problem is that everything changes!

Our emotions are often linked to limiting beliefs that prevent us from being able to access a higher consciousness. Fiona Taylor believes it is essential to transform this emotional charge into something positive: "In assisting athletes to get focused many are taught to control their own thoughts. Some athletes are better at doing this than others. The focus in sports psychology has largely been on controlling thoughts, or using the power of the mind to focus and override negative or self-sabotaging thoughts. However, feelings underpin thoughts. You cannot change a feeling by using positive thoughts to override it. The only way you can change a feeling is to change your perceptions and awareness about the issues relating to the particular feeling. In other words we must find the origin of the feeling itself. We must understand why we feel a certain way in the first place. The only way to change a limiting belief that resides in our subconscious or unconscious mind is to find the ultimate cause and origin of the feeling and belief. You can try and not feel a feeling, however if you ignore it, it does not mean the feeling has gone away."

We must learn to become aware of our emotions, but also how to interpret and understand them. Only then we can use them to our advantage. Christian Target,[53] in his attempt to describe what he also calls flow states, highlights the key role of emotions. For him it is essential to optimize this focus on the feelings. And this is possible through our emotions. Emotions will tap into the appropriate energy level to fill the needs of the moment. And to prepare the best ground for emotions, he naturally suggests visualization and relaxation, both rooted in optimal physical preparation. Here we find again mind–body interaction.

Finally, a third link among all the ingredients allowing us to reach the Zone is something that recurs in every description: the practice of meditation. Jerry Lynch notes that "I am not a researcher but I am in 'the trenches' with athletes and I have no answers . . . just observations after 35 years of work in the field. What I notice is that meditation creates an inner environment where the athlete increases the chances for the Zone to take place. There is no actual thinking; it relies on intuitive responses (instinct), being calm, focusing only on what can be controlled and letting go of outcomes, result, scores—the things that cannot be controlled. I notice that once an athlete begins to notice that he/she is 'in the Zone,' it no longer exists."[54] Many athletes have indeed understood this, including Korean archers—among the best in the world in the 1980s—who incorporated several hours of meditation into their daily training.

In the Western world, however, meditation is not taken very seriously. Some still think it cuts an athlete off from reality. But as pointed out by Peter Spang, a former tennis professional, maybe the main problem is that "nobody has a copyright on meditation! It is accessible to everybody."[55] Spang is one of the few who have tried the approach of Tim Gallwey, the "Inner Game." He simply saw tennis as a golden opportunity for a certain form of Zen meditation, as archery was for Herrigel.

Michael Lardon has worked with athletes who are among the best in the world, and discovered that the brain produces the same type of waves during meditation and Zone. Dr. John Douillard has reached similar conclusions: "The most remarkable finding is the reproduction of alpha brain wave during exercise, indicating a state of inner calm. The mind is composed, the body is functioning in an efficient, relaxed way—in the midst of the most dynamic physical activity. The athlete is doing less and accomplishing more. Alpha is usually found during sleep, deep states of relaxation, biofeedback, and meditation. What is so unusual about the alpha [waves] in the Zone is that they are produced during exercise. Yet they are characteristic of a style of functioning in which thoughts are minimal, and mind and body are relaxed. This seems to be the neurophysiological correlate of what athletes sometimes call the 'mindless state,' where everything just happens and you're not thinking about it."[56] Some argue that if athletes are able to switch to alpha waves, they will be able to slide naturally into the Zone. Coaches can help their athletes create a better mind–body integration naturally by learning to breathe better via the practice of meditation.

Feed your dreams.

Make a dream board.

Every day take five minutes to visualize yourself where you want to be. See yourself there. Feel the emotions you would like to live.

Always take time to meditate, especially when you don't have time for it.

Take the time to read *Finding your Zone* by Mike Lardon.

I take time for meditation.
I pursue my dreams.

The missing piece

The spirit of a Being is reflected in his eyes
and in all movements and gestures of his body.
—Kahlil Gibran

The soul understands what the mind cannot conceive.
—Neale Donald Walsh

Forty-some years ago Michael Murphy wrote *Golf in the Kingdom,*[57] a story revealing the connection between sports and the spiritual dimension. Shortly after the book's publication, Murphy began receiving calls and letters from athletes telling him amazing stories about inexplicable experiences in their sports. This inexplicable dimension doesn't appear in academic studies. Yet it is far more common than we might imagine. Sadaharu Oh, for example, one of baseball's greatest batters, described the Zone in spiritual terms.[58] More recently Fiona Taylor has given her vision of the Zone: "The ultimate state of the Zone is actually a state of being where we are fully connected with spiritual intuition combined with emotions, the missing ingredient in many training programs."

In the first part of this book I talked about the hundreds of testimonials[59] collected in the late 1970s by Mike Murphy. He emphasized the importance of the spiritual side in these stories: "This is not to say that athletes are yogis or mystics. Very few of us approach games with the lifelong dedication and conscious aspiration for enlightenment that the mystical path requires. It is simply to recognize that similarities exist between the two fields of activity, both in their methods and in the states they evoke. The many reports we have collected show us that sport has enormous power to sweep us beyond our ordinary sense of self, to evoke capacities that have generally been regarded as mystical or spiritual."

Andrew Cooper, a journalist who has long studied Zen and Tai Chi and authored *Playing in the Zone,* speaks of "the hidden dimension of sport,"[60] because athletes rarely speak of this facet of the Zone. Most people have trouble accepting the spiritual side of the Zone because they have no context to understand it, no language or philosophy to support it. At the end of his career, Bill Russell recalled the "mystic feeling" that he had never spoken of before: "The subject was taboo, and he knew that breaking that taboo would invite the mockery of his peers." Has the situation changed since then? Not really, and that's why former NFL player Dave Meggyesy says that the psychology of sports training is incomplete because it ignores an essential part of the athlete's experience: the spiritual side.

Reflections about the spiritual side of sports can at first seem a bit strange. We can doubt or laugh, but this view is finding its way into popular thought. Recently Mike Lardon made the connection very clearly. According to Lardon, we can develop the high-level awareness associated with the Zone in "various ways including physical training, meditation, mental training, and spiritual practices." This path to the Zone will probably require more time to see full acceptance.

What is your inner drive for your sport?

What has been your primary motivating force since you were a kid?

Take the time to read *Spirit in Sport* by Fiona Taylor.

I give thanks for every beautiful moment.

Connection

We are shaped and fashioned by what we love.
—Johann Wolfgang von Goethe

The spiritual aspects of sports and the Zone are often described by athletes in terms of feeling connected to something greater than themselves. We can find this idea of connection in Peter Nabokov's book *Indian Running*,[61] an exploration into the traditions of Native American runners, which shows that they are part of a spiritual framework. Ancient cultures and spiritual practices have long honored the connection between a higher intelligence and the human ability to perform, endure, or overcome.

The Zone may therefore be a matter of connection—but not only at the brain level! Terry Orlick agrees, stating: "One of the greatest lessons that I have learned from great performers is the oneness or absolute connection that they have with what they are doing, seeing, feeling, or creating."

By letting our intuition guide us, we can feel and

strengthen this connection. But for the untrained, it can be fragile, and what takes us away from this connection is to think, to question, or to judge. There is a time to analyze, but there is also a time to fully connect with what we do. We need to learn to recognize the presence of the Zone so we're not surprised, we're not separated from the action, and we don't lose the connection, but rather embrace it.

This connection isn't merely an individual experience; it can be shared. Australian rower and triple Olympic champion Drew Ginn understood this and pointed out that the Zone can involve two or more people, or occur between a person and an object. It can also be experienced between an athlete and an animal, as seen in equestrian sports, or an athlete and nature, as surfers often report.

Sports psychologist Nathalie Crepin believes that "this state is also found in team sports. Then a group acts united, gestures are accurate, errors almost don't exist and the technical and tactical choices are the best. There emerges from the whole group a sense of harmony and invincibility."[62] And this connection can go beyond the team, as underlined by Mike Murphy: "Not only are individual players or whole teams transported at peak moments, but this ecstasy can be shared by fans." A feeling also reported by Chris Evert: "You feel one with the fans. You don't feel like you're on the court and the fans are cheering, you don't feel like they're separate from you. You just feel at one and at peace with the whole scene."

By discipline, training, and mastery, this exploration into the Zone shows us that sometimes the consciousness of the player seems to make a qualitative jump to another level. In her book *Spirit in Sport,* Fiona Taylor interviews many champions and highlights the ways that our ability to experience the Zone and reproduce this moment are linked to our level of consciousness: "I postulate that the ability to experience the zone in sport, and reproduce optimal states of performance over and over again, relates to a person's level of consciousness. The more spiritually evolved we are, the higher our consciousness level. The more we can access power at the universal or spiritual level, the more we can access the zone."[63]

Few have dared to bring this argument into sports, but if we review our study from the beginning, there is a missing piece in the "Zone puzzle." The spiritual aspect may therefore be a good road to explore, especially when champions are beginning to emphasize its importance. A credible example is Mark Allen, winner of six Ironman competitions —considered one of the toughest in sports. Though he's among the best triathletes in the world, Allen struggled to break the barrier that prevented him to win the grueling triathlon in Kona, Hawaii. He began studying with Brant Secunda, shaman from the Huichol Indian tradition (Mexico). Brant taught Mark spiritual and healing exercises that allowed him to integrate his physical and psychological sides. The result speaks for itself: Allen won six Ironmans in six appearances, a record never achieved before. He credits Secunda's teaching for his victories. For Allen, it was the time he spent with the shaman that allowed him to pass "the test of body and soul." After learning how to simultaneously train both mind and body, he now teaches athletes to integrate the full spectrum of body, heart, and spirit into sport. Allen and Secunda have detailed their experiences in a book[64] and provided practical tools that can be adapted to our lifestyle. For them, the foundation is emotional and spiritual well-being;

therefore they work primarily within these two fields. They highlight spirituality as the missing piece we need to find our inspiration and be completely committed. Their philosophy is simply to find the connection between the physical body and the soul, a connection that has diminished more in modern times.

An academic study supporting this notion was surprisingly conducted by Kathleen Dillon and Jennifer Tait from the University of California–Davis. Their research indicates a psychological link between the state of the Zone and the spiritual dimension.[65] Athletes participated in two tests in order to measure the spiritual nature of their sport experience and to evaluate if they showed characteristics of the Zone. Results from the two tests appeared to be significantly related, giving empirical validation to the relationship between spirituality and the Zone. Also approaching the Zone scientifically, Mike Lardon came to the same conclusion: "It is often the heart and soul of a person, those elements invisible and untouchable, which are determinants." A strong argument from someone who has studied this phenomenon for over thirty years!

Pay attention to the connections around you; they can be a great source of energy.

Remember the last time you watched your favorite champion. Remember the energy you felt. You knew this athlete was in the Zone.

Feed your dream with this energy.

Whatever it represents for you, the missing piece is spirit—your inner experience of the universe.

Reconnect to your higher self, mind, body, and spirit.

Once you are there, you won't be alone anymore.

Take the time to read *Fit Soul, Fit Body* by Brant Secunda and Mark Allen.

Inspiration can be found wherever I look.

To do it

Absorb what is useful. Research your own experience.
—Bruce Lee

The Zone requires a delicate balance between control and flexibility, voluntary effort and letting go, conscious thoughts and instinctive performance. It is *not* the result of abstract intellectual concepts, but rather a momentary fusion of experience, body, mind, and emotions.

In the Zone we are moving from a learning or training mode to trusting our inner self. It requires confidence in our body and its capabilities.

A mind–body training program could therefore include meditation, visual imagery, and the development of sensory and kinesthetic awareness. Fran Pirozzolo, mental trainer of the Texas Rangers baseball team, thinks many coaching programs would benefit from the development of our sensory awareness: "The importance of vision and kinesthetic sense are of the utmost importance to reach the Zone. They are probably two gold mines for the future! To be interested in the Zone is inevitably to stumble upon the most important issues in sports, motor learning and memory . . . [These] would allow athletes to grow, learn and perform better."

In summary, the best advice for creating the physiological and mental conditions conducive to the Zone would be to *change our attention* and *become aware of our body posture and breathing*. Both promote a leap of consciousness, and both are favored by the practice of meditation.

This is the exact approach of Ronan Lafaix, former coach of tennis pro Stéphane Robert, who reached the sixty-first ATP ranking in 2010. In his fascinating book[66] Lafaix highlights the importance of breathing, and of grounding our sensory awareness in the present. For him it all starts with routines and rituals that involve our senses, thus creating a heightened awareness of both body and mind. Relaxation and meditation help athletes improve their mental images of their own bodies and sensations. To anchor these sensations, Lafaix gives special attention to posture. Then it is necessary to bring emotions, heart, and intuition into play to strengthen the anchor. Lafaix is probably one of the only top coaches to have implemented high-level methods and techniques based on Tim Gallwey's approach.

Here we perhaps shouldn't use the word *technique*—because is breathing a technique? No, it is more a means to *guide an athlete to into using what is already within.* Just taking the time to ground the body, to breathe, and to observe both mind and environment, Lafaix helps players know themselves better, finding the right concentration, finding their own rhythm. It's a pace very different from that dictated by scientifically overloaded training programs that often forget we are not robots. Nobody had really tried this approach before. With Stéphane Robert they have dared to do it. And it works! Is this just luck? Certainly not, as Lafaix's approach is linked to several centuries of trusted techniques and practices. The success of Phil Jackson's Chicago Bulls and now the Lakers may break the misconception that practices such as meditation are not compatible with high-level competition. A way is now open. It's a way that many are still struggling to fully see, but it has already aroused a lot of curiosity. And to be curious, to wonder, is already a window to the Zone!

Trust your skills, your body, and your mind.

Meditate, visualize, and develop your body awareness.

Breathing and posture are the pillars.

Take the time to find one or two routines
that really fit your body, mind, and spirit.
Once you've chosen them,
repeat them again and again!

What in your sport makes you grow?

Every experience is something I can learn from.

Don't think, feel!

Come, seize the present moment in joy.
—Omar Khayyám

I run as I feel.
—Henry Rono

Passion is the creativity of life.
It allows us to do everything with love.
—Hélène Grimaud

After this overview, the paths to the Zone are drawn. It's up to you to choose: the scientific approach, the Eastern approach, or a mixture of both? From who or what will come the biggest breakthrough? From advances in neuroscience? From sports psychology? Maybe just from athletes themselves, now better prepared for Zone experiences and therefore better able to describe them.

Who will dare to think outside the box and start from a

very young age to really work on both body and mind, and finally end this era dominated by the physical and biomechanics? Men like Mike Murphy or Tim Gallwey have tried it, but they were ahead of their time—too far ahead, maybe. But now it is in the air. Fifteen years ago, some thought[67] we were witnessing the birth of a unified approach, a fusion between the best of the East and the West. This birth is a bit laborious, but we can see some progress. Phil Jackson, Jerry Lynch, and Ronan Lafaix have shown that it is possible, even in ultracompetitive high-performance sports. This method of coaching aims to help athletes or teams access their own Zone.

People are looking for a magic pill or a secret formula that could replicate the harmony found in the Zone. But if we look at everything clearly, the most surprising question is not how we find the Zone; rather, it is this: Given our incredible potential, why are we in it so rarely? This echoes the view of Falk Mieschendahl, a yoga and mediation teacher: "The Zone is always here and now, but one cannot do it. The reason . . . is that you cannot do what you already are. You can only uncover it, dust off the noise on top of it, and flow with what happens. In a way, it is getting out of the way"—much the way a great painter or skilled author gets out of the way and draws from what is within. "The meeting of this superfluous state with skill (whatever this skill may be—physical, intellectual, creative, etc.) creates 'beauty' on an intrinsic level as well as on an extrinsic level (at least most of the time)."[68]

The Zone is not a magical place. It is something that we all have within us but may have forgotten. We just need to rediscover it.

Only two or three pioneers in the last thirty years have dared to name what is lacking in all our techniques: soul, passion, and love of what we do. This may seem a bit simplistic, but what made us all persevere, spending countless hours in training? Yes, love of our sport—the love of the game and the feelings it provides us! So after all these assumptions about this elusive Zone, one thing is sure: *If you do something you love deep inside, then your chances of finding the Zone will increase!*

Many have felt this incredible energy, which leads us and makes us say: "I love it," "I'm here for that," or "I never thought about doing something else." That is the message of the great baseball player of the 1970s, Sadaharu Oh: "My baseball career was a long, long initiation into a single secret:

At the heart of all things is love." And that of golf champion Johnny Miller: "I think love is the secret. I think it's love that gets you in the zone. I really believe it. If you really love to do what you're doing and you want to share your skills with the people watching you and those around you and love the course and just can't wait to play it, it's going to be fun."

Now, as athletes, what can we expect from our ability to enter the Zone, or as coaches from helping athletes reach the Zone? Obviously, the phenomenon has not yet been studied long-term or at high levels. There is still a long way to go, but in some areas (such as vision and body awareness) we have made good progress. It is time to discover not only what allows us to be in the Zone but how *not* to lose our connection to it. What makes the subject really exciting is that beyond the chemical and biological causes, these experiences touch our consciousness, an almost virgin field of research.

These new discoveries give the Zone even more meaning and help us see our own huge and untapped potential. These are the keys that open our inner experiences and help us evolve and grow. Thus, sometimes touching the world of the Zone, athletes become more curious. This search often leads them to discover new techniques, broaden their horizons, and learn how to better connect body and mind. And often their performance improves. If sport is at the root of this transformation, what guides athletes is more than just passion for their sport. It is the desire to evolve, the desire to grow, the desire to expand beyond expectations. Yes, though some still have doubts, sport allows us to express our ultimate best!

Don't think outside the box.
Think like there is no box!

Be yourself.

During tough times, never forget that
your Zone is always here and now.

Play from what is within.

Rediscover the first joy you experienced
in your sport.

Remember your smile, your energy.
Remember what made you think:
I'm here for that!

Take the time to read *The Power of Now*
by Eckhart Tolle.

I keep learning.
I keep going.
I keep my mind open.

The boy reached through to the Soul of the World, and saw that it was part of the Soul of God. And he saw that the Soul of God was his own soul.

And that he, the boy, could perform miracles.

—Paulo Coelho, *The Alchemist*

Endnotes

1. We can find other terms in the literature: *white moments, exercise high, runner's high, in the groove, in my world,* or *locked in.*

2. Andrew Cooper (2008), *Playing in the Zone: Exploring the Spiritual Dimensions of Sports,* Shambhala Publications.

3. See some good testimonials in Hubert Ripoll (2008), *Le Mental des Champions: Comprendre la Réussite Sportive,* Editions Payot.

4. Charlie Jones (1997), *What Makes Winners Win: Over 100 Athletes, Coaches, and Managers Tell You the Secrets of Success,* Broadway Books.

5. *New York Times,* April 9, 1989.

6. Susan A. Jackson and Mihaly Csikszentmihalyi (1999), *Flow in Sports: The Keys to Optimal Experiences and Performances,* Human Kinetics.

7. See Jean-Philippe Vaillant (2008), *Tennis: Pensez Comme un Champion,* Editions Amphora.

8. Shane M. Murphy and Annemarie Infantino Murphy (2009), "How to Reach Your Sports Zone," www.selfhelp-magazine.com/article/sports-zone.

9. Daniel Goleman (1999), *L'Intelligence Émotionnelle,* Editions Robert Laffont.

10. Christine Le Scanff, (1995). *La Conscience Modifiée,* Editions Payot.

11. John Douillard (1994), *Body, Mind, and Sport,* Three Rivers Press.

12. Thomas Gilovich, Robert Vallone, and Amos Tversky (1985), "The Hot Hand in Basketball: On the Misperception of Random Sequences," *Cognitive Psychology* 17, 295–314.

13. Janet Young and Michelle Pain (1999), *The Zone: Evidence of a Universal Phenomenon for Athletes Across Sports,* Monash University, Australia.

14. Ripoll, *Le Mental des Champions.*

15. Murphy and White, *In the Zone.*

16. *Radio Classique: Passion Classique,* February 25, 2010.

17. Goleman, *L'Intelligence Émotionnelle.*

18. Ripoll, *Mental des Champions.*

19. Le Scanff, *Conscience Modifiée.*

20. John Gorrie (2009), *Performing in the Zone,* www.thezonebook.com.

21. www.tennis-in-the-zone.com.

22. Damien Lafont (2008), "Gaze Control During the Hitting Phase in Tennis: A Preliminary Study," *International Journal of Performance Analysis in Sport* 8(1), 85–100; ibid. (2007), "Towards a New Hitting Model in Tennis," *International Journal of Performance Analysis in Sport* 7(3), 106–116.

23. Kazumi Tabata (2003), *Secret Tactics,* Tuttle Publishing.

24. Vaillant, *Tennis.*

25. George Leonard (1974), *The Ultimate Athlete,* North Atlantic Books.

26. Tim Gallwey (1974), *The Inner Game of Tennis,* Random House.

27. Ibid.

28. Vaillant, *Tennis.*

29. Denis Grozdanovitch (2007), *De L'Art de Prendre la Balle au Rebond,* Editions J. C. Lattès.

30. "Lettre Ouverte à un Sportif sur le Style," in *Les Chemins de L'Écriture,* Grasset, 1942.

31. Terry Orlick (2008), *In Pursuit of Excellence,* Human Kinetics.

32. Joe Parent (2002), *Zen Golf,* Random House.

33. Among them is Phil Jackson (1996), *Sacred Hoops,* Hyperion.

34. Henry Abbott, June 16, 2010, ESPN.

35. Michael Maccoby, *Washington Post,* June 15, 2009.

36. Ross Robertson, interview, "The Soul of Team Work," www.enlightennext.org.

37. Richard Hoffer, *Sport Illustrated,* May 27, 1996.

38. Mihaly Csikszentmihalyi (1991), *Flow: The Psychology of Optimal Experience,* HarperCollins Publishers.

39. Daisetz T. Suzuki (2010), *Zen and Japanese Culture,* Princeton University Press.

40. Michael Lardon (2008), *Finding Your Zone,* Perigee Books.

41. Parent, *Zen Golf.*

42. Dan Millman (1994), *The Inner Athlete,* Stillpoint.

43. Dan Millman, *The Peaceful Warrior.* DVD.

44. Bill Russell (1980), *Second Wind,* Ballantine Books.

45. Fiona Taylor (2007), *Spirit in Sport: Peak Performance and the Zone in Sport,* Barakaya.

46. Ibid.

47. Douillard, *Body, Mind, and Sport.*

48. Roy Palmer (2006), *Zone Mind, Zone Body,* Ecademy Press.

49. Eugen Herrigel (1953, 1981), *Zen in the Art of Archery,* Random House.

50. Jerry Lynch and Chungliang Al Huang (2006), *The Way of the Champion,* Tuttle Publishing; wayofchampions.com.

51. Lardon, *Finding Your Zone.*

52. Charlie Jones (1997), *What Makes Winners Win,* Broadway Books.

53. Christian Target (2002), *Manuel de Préparation Mentale,* Editions Chiron.

54. Lynch and Chungliang, *Way of the Champion.*

55. Peter Spang (1998), *Zennis*, Perigee.

56. Douillard, *Body, Mind, and Sport*.

57. Michael Murphy (1997), *Golf in the Kingdom*, Penguin.

58. Sadaharu Oh (1985), *A Zen Way of Baseball*, Vintage.

59. Murphy and White, *In the Zon*.

60. Cooper, *Playing in the Zone*.

61. Peter Nabokov (1987), *Indian Running*, Ancient City Press.

62. Le Flow ou L'État Optimal de Performance, à la Recherche du Graal (2007), www.irbms.com.

63. Taylor, *Spirit in Sport*.

64. Mark Allen and Brant Secunda (2010), *Fit Soul, Fit Body*, BenBella Books.

65. K. Dillon and J. Tait (2000), "Spirtituality and Being in the Zone in Team Sports: A Relationship? *Journal of Sport Behavior*, 23.

66. Ronan Lafaix (2008), *Tennis—Soyez P.R.O.*, Editions Amphora.

67. Tony Schwartz (1995), *What Really Matters*, Bantam Books.

68. www.humanflow.de.

Other titles of interest from Breakaway Books